ELLEN NEWTON was born in Melbourne, Australia, in 1896, the daughter of a well-known criminal lawyer. Educated at boarding school and at Melbourne University, she began to write as soon as she could spell. Throughout her long life she has been a freelance writer, broadcaster and short-story writer, and has worked in libraries and bookshops. In her seventies, suffering from angina, Ellen Newton spent six years in a series of nursing homes, years she laboriously recorded in her secret diary. At the age of 81, she rebelled. Being of sound mind, she discharged herself from hospital, with the help of her family found a small flat where she still happily lives, and prepared her diary for publication. She is now working on her first novel.

THIS BED MY CENTRE

ELLEN NEWTON

Virago

Published by VIRAGO Limited 1980
5 Wardour Street, London W1V 3HE

First published in Australia by
McPhee Gribble Publishers 1979

Copyright © Ellen Newton 1979

ISBN 0 86068 147 5

Printed by The Anchor Press Ltd and
bound by Wm Brendon & Son Ltd
both of Tiptree, Essex

CONTENTS

INTRODUCTION

This diary began in despair... It soon became my close companion and gradually grew into a book. It tells of traumatic years that should never have happened. There was another way.

Nothing in the diary is invented, though names of people and places are changed. Incidents and conversations are set down exactly as they happened, sometimes while they were actually happening. Gaps here and there, sometimes of days, sometimes of months, are due to illness, intrusive curiosity as to what I was writing about, and some editing at a later stage to improve the narrative. Very often I wrote in the small hours, and in the morning, in pencil, mostly, on salvaged spare pages of notebooks and the backs of used envelopes. These bits and pieces were scattered in bags and boxes for want of a desk to hold them. There was no thought whatever of publication.

One solitary afternoon, reading these fragments at random, it seemed that my writing might help other segregated men and women – who are mentally alert, even creative, though elderly or handicapped by illness – not just to stay alive, but to live. By that thing called chance, help came from the Australia Council and with it a plentiful supply of paper, pens and paper-fasteners. A long-standing friend generously offered to investigate the possibilities of publication.

This diary began in despair – but it ended in hope. Long years of unnatural waiting in places surrounded by death threatened to overwhelm me. Despair is a grim denial of life. And I could no longer go on fighting it.

Was there nowhere to live where fresh air was not taboo, where one could walk fifty yards without meeting obstacles along the way? I managed, after tactful enquiry, to discover that, if you are of sound mind, you can, at any time, discharge yourself from hospital without medical consent. But how?

Certainly, it had to be without melodrama. And the responsibility must be all mine. I might live six days, six weeks or six years out of hospital. But at least it would be Me – not 'the one in ward 7'.

Helen was my biggest hurdle. At last I convinced her that I wasn't courting voluntary euthanasia, and that anyone who could write a book and find a publisher should be able to live like an ordinary human being. She agreed to try and find me a small flat. That is where I'm writing now, alone, but happy, independent, and of some use in the world.

For all this my thanks go to my doctors whose skill and compassion brought me to the point of return, and for their care and encouragement, too, that keep me on the escape-route. I thank the Australia Council, especially Dr Michael Costigan and Miss Pat Healy, for their quick perception and kindness, and also my very understanding publishers. Above all my thanks for her endless thought and caring go to my one and only Helen.

E.M.N.
February 1979

PRINCE EDWARD'S

April

Tuesday You can be gay without frivolity, my old history teacher used to remind me. I thought of her on this afternoon of sun and gentle breezes. My heart was singing in its own special weather.

Prince Edward's, and three months of intensive care, comfort and humour, from Matron to the youngest nursing-aide, had got me on my feet. 'They always get you on your feet,' said my handsome cardiologist, playing down his own star-part as he usually does.

Three more turns up and down the balcony. Then once around the corner. That makes five. Home on Thursday must be a certainty. He said 'as soon as you can walk'. The wind combs through my hair. Over my shoulder the elms are waving a ribbon of green round the Fitzroy Gardens. Sister calls me. Not unsteadily I go inside. This must be my G.P. coming to tell me when I can go.

No questions. No examination. For all his Dior tie and shocking pink shirt to match, he seems edgy. He's wasting no time on me today.

'Miss Newton.' Pause. Then, 'Mrs Zachary's blood pressure has gone up pretty high.'

Yesterday Helen seemed well enough.

'Doctor, is she very ill?'

'No. But it could be serious. If it got really high, she could have a stroke.' He fixes me with his eyes, in the way he probably looks at his small children when he promises just what will happen to them, if they disobey.

My heart knocks at my ribs.

'Doctor, is she likely to have a stroke?'

After a pause, he says, 'No.'

If only I could be home with Helen, now. She must need someone to take care of her.

'Your sister feels she can't stand the strain of your long illness.' Then another of his Grand Pauses.

I've often thought how much harder it must be for Helen to stand by me in all my alarms and excursions than it is for me to live through them. But why didn't she tell me herself? Why must she leave it to him to tell me?

'We've decided it will be best for you to live in a nursing home where you will get the expert care you need.' *We've decided.* Angels would have trodden more warily. So would Matron. And clever, downright Sister Mead could have told this highly qualified young doctor that they might at least have given me a small voice in their decision to wrap up my life forever. There were things I might have said, too, if I hadn't suddenly felt tired, and as cold as buried stone.

And why, oh why must he wear that shocking pink today?

'It will be better if you do not go home,' he says, just like a clerk at a tourist bureau saying you'll do better travelling in the Southern Aurora, than in the Daylight Express. Home is your peculiar treasure. For your G.P. it is just another address. You are no longer an average human being, alive with joys and doubts and fears. Hope is not for you, either. From today you are a Patient.

'We've arranged for you to go straight from here on Thursday to Haddon – the nursing home where we've booked you in.'

As quickly as that, he had stripped all brightness from the day.

'It will be better, you know, if you don't go home at all from here.'

'Yes, Doctor.'

He left me – with my future foretold. Without another word. When he closed the door, it was just like the finality of death.

Someone has said there's no cure for birth and death, except to enjoy the interval. Well the lights must go up for me, too. And after all, my interval may not be a very long one. But *Haddon*? To me it's more remote than the Kimberleys. But then the whole situation is unreal. Not that I can't grasp that something like it must one day happen. What I can't believe is that Helen, the very core of my heart, could let it happen this way. The sunlit breeze still spills through the balcony door and windows, so that the curtains move in their forest greens and browns as if they were alive.

Sister Mead, after what she probably thinks is time enough for me to get my bearings, opens the door.

'So you are leaving us on Thursday? Just take it in your stride. I'll be out to see you one day.'

'Have you ever heard of Haddon, Sister?'

'No, I really don't think I have.'

'It's one of those nursing homes where old ladies go to die...'

'Now, listen to me, my dear. Even if you were a twenty-year-old, with a heart and blood condition that needs constant professional care, there's simply nowhere else for you to go.'

Older and more perceptive than my overworked G.P., Sister reminds me that I will have a private room at Haddon. But 'a room of one's own' in a

THIS BED MY CENTRE

nursing home affords me little delight.

'Time you were back in bed,' says Sister, plumping up the pillows. 'I'll see you in the morning.'

The balcony door is open wide. It cuts out a crane swinging above the skeleton top storey of a new high-rise across the way. The crane and the man on top look just like a piece in a jigsaw puzzle. Half a dozen of these steel and concrete boxes cut dreary abstracts on the skyline. They leave no space for the sun to throw a golden shaft across the footpath. And there are no gaps for the wind to sweep away smog that sometimes spreads to the hills, from the city and nearby, industrial suburbs. Yet sometimes, just before daybreak, I've watched these monsters change for a few moments into a Whistler Nocturne... Not the least good thing about my six pillows is that they let me see the Dandenongs, blue in the far distance, from the window at the foot of my bed.

'How are you, m'dear?' It is Matron, looking incredibly young for the load she carries. She has beautiful eyes, warm, compassionate, and deep hyacinth-blue. She wears her well-cut uniform with an air and is nothing if not forthright, and that, too, is part of her charm.

'So you're leaving us, m'dear?'

'The day after tomorrow. Matron, do you know Haddon?'

No, I didn't think she would.

'But don't you forget,' she says, 'if ever you need us, there will always be a room here for you.' Her hand closes firmly over mine and she is gone. I reach for the squiggle pad that Julia brought me from Scotland. I don't know why, but I begin to write everything that has happened to me this afternoon, without changing a word. As the hours go by I wish I hadn't been

6

blessed with such a memory.

This is a day without end. As it crawls into night, sleep defies me. The hot drink and set of tranquillizers brought me a couple of hours ago by the best of all night nurses haven't even made me drowsy. Nurse is big, safe and comforting. Everything about her is generous. She is a well of sense and gentle humour. This is my sixth retreat to Prince Edward's, and she has helped me over a good many thorny patches. When the floor is quiet, she makes time for a quick word with me about a piece of old china she has bought – or a vintage record she has unearthed of matchless Lotte Lehmann in *Rosenkavalier*. But tonight, she is needed elsewhere.

Sleep. But you can't, with your thoughts monotonously turning and turning, like a merry-go-round. This must be what it means to be dispossessed. But how does one live, sealed off in a vacuum from everyday things – the joys and hopes and fears that come from being not just one of the family but really part of it? No more of those tremendous trifles like sitting together by the T.V., sherry in hand, waiting for the evening news. No more talk of the day's doings over the lively meal that follows, a meal with a special savour of its own because it is shared.

Somewhere in the distance a clock strikes three. *Never, Never, Never* come for pity. You are only crowning this despair, you know, by heaping up remembrance of these happy yesterdays. Yet this could go on for years. To have come so far you must be as tough as a mountain goat. Besides, both your grandmothers, in the picturesque, unhygienic days of Victoria and Edward, and the better days of the two Georges, lived every minute of their lives till they were all but a hundred years old.

Nurse with her tray of tea, lemon, and little triangles of bread and butter as thin as leaves: 'Morning
tea is early today,' she says, with a twinkle. 'Have it
now, and then go off to sleep.' There's comfort in tea,
at this hour of a long night.

My G.P. did his best. He didn't know he was
ruthless, but he was right. Widowed early, Helen has
given half a life-time to her children, and lately, very
much of it to me. To have illness setting her pattern
for living would never do. She must have freedom to
go her own lively way. This way is best for her, and it
must be made to appear best.

Nurse takes away the tray. 'Not asleep yet?'

If only I were. It's strangely quiet – not even the
wail of a police siren or an ambulance for hours. You
could hear a leaf fall. But it was Helen, always so
good at making quick decisions, who in the first
place wanted us to live together. She doesn't think
that for me living is going to mean one bleak, aseptic,
whitewalled room or another to the very end. One
room to be my everywhere. There's no choice.
Acceptance is not enough. I have to find a technique
to fit this sentence of living. Even the bitterness of
death passes if you think of it as setting you free.

Morning begins to grope its way over a misty sky.
In my heart it is raining. Then at last, heavy,
undreaming sleep.

Wednesday ◢ Out of the early mist comes another
golden autumn day that makes you think of deep
purple grapes and Macedon's copper beeches. Sister
Mead brings me the programme of *Giselle*. Ballet and
symphony concerts are meat and drink to her, too.
With pithy comments, she lets me share them by
proxy. Sister is her own person, and fully aware that
she is the uncrowned queen of this floor. A quick,

small-boned woman, no longer young, she flashes in and out of my room like a bird, bringing comfort always, and making me feel that in her hands I must be safe. Because of her, fear of angina is not one of my problems. She was with me that first time. So calm, so quick and so deft with the injection to kill the pain, that stabs like a nerve in a stricken tooth. Because she said so, you knew that the clutching, clamping chest-pain that stifled you, would soon be over, too. I didn't know then, that angina comes back again. And again.

Afternoon brings Helen, laden with oranges, black olives and champagne – my favourite tipple.

'I'm proud of you,' says Helen.

'No comment, darling,' is my firm reply.

'*Very* proud of you.'

'Helen, darling, *positively*, no comment.'

And so back to the smoother surface of things, and we're on the old, everyday footing again.

Soon it will be dusk. Sipping the champagne, I think of the long, happy give and take between us – all the little nameless things that make up the small change of happiness. Stop. Helen would be appalled to think her good champagne could be used to lace regret.

My pocket-sized transistor is tuned to Bach's lovely *Air in G.* The windows let in the spires and part of the roof – gargoyles and all – and a glimpse of stained glass – of the Australian-Gothic Cathedral poised in its bluestone majesty on the crest of the hill. It has great beauty when it is floodlit. But when it swims in moonlight it takes on the exquisite, elusive quality of a dream. The Cathedral goes well with Bach.

Thursday ∅ Awake early, though the day is not to be as planned. Today all brightness has fallen from

9

the air. Suntanned, young nursing-aide Debbie beams – and sometimes raises an eyebrow – as she packs my serendipity suitcase.

'I'll bet you've had an interesting life, Miss Newton,' she says.

'Yes, it has been – here and there. But what makes you think so, Nurse?' She laughs.

'Oh, because you never talk about illness.' As I watch her, a long forgotten story, read when I was all of eight years old, comes slowly back to me, by a fantastic quirk of memory. It was in one of those hefty, cloth bound, yearly volumes of *The Strand* or *The Windsor Magazine* that used to be found in most well-conducted, suburban homes. The story was about a princess. In those days a princess was almost as seductive as a witch, or a dragon. This princess had forebodings. So she wrote a letter:

'I wish,' the letter said, 'to be buried in my best red velvet gown, with my doll, Nancy, beside me.'

'My best gown.' Yes, of course. In my most presentable housecoat, unfortunately not red velvet, but quite good, my mirror tells me, I make myself ready. In my hand, my much-travelled 'Week-End Book' is a substitute for that royal doll, Nancy. After a struggle, my suitcase reluctantly closes. Three months in hospital have begotten a hoard of mysteriously desirable bits and pieces. Ribbons, books, cards with reproductions of great paintings. Boxes, empty, but too attractive to throw away. They amaze even a born collector like me. But in they go.

A smooth streamlined wheel-chair stands ready. Helen walks on one side, weighed down with books and a bird's nest of a basket full of odd-shaped little boxes and phials that could add a colour or two to the rainbow, and would be a bower bird's delight. Sister is on the other side, with my letter of introduction to Haddon. Nurse steers me to the lift. Then down, and in an instant we are at the car, parked squarely across the main entrance.

Fixing rug and cushions more to her liking, Sister says, 'I'll be out to see you before long, my dear.'

Matron comes from her office to wish me well.

My heart is beating like a drum.

'Let's go,' says Helen. The old, quick smile is reflected in her grey eyes that seem to hold tenderness for all the world. With a wave of hands and one last look back, we are on our way. Something of the affection and the spirit of Prince Edward's seems to go with me.

HADDON

May

Friday As we drove past the Gardens and on to the freeway, I made myself a promise. Come wind, come wrack, there would be no more drama. Haddon it would be, until my final destination. Everyone has inside himself one piece of good news. I think Ugo Betti said that. But no matter who did, it's a thought to cherish.

We stopped at a low iron gate. A short path from it to a rambling, old, white timber villa. Helen went through the gate. Soon a friendly young sister appeared, trundling a decrepit invalid chair. It wasn't really cold, but the nurse's scarlet cape underlined her dark prettiness in a way that gave her the best of reasons for wearing it. She may have been celebrating her last day at Haddon, for I never saw her again.

The wheels of the old chair baulked at first at the three steps that joined the path to the verandah. It gave me time to see a vast side lawn that badly needed cutting, bordered by two narrow beds knee-high in weeds. There was a bird bath too, with strips of chalky white paint dripping from it, and in the middle, a little broken-nosed cupid. Beside the verandah, a freshly raked bed and a camellia with a few tight buds. It looked unloved. A massive cypress hedge, about twenty feet high, stretching across the entire frontage, didn't help.

There was another stop before we crossed the dazzling brass-plated doorstep into the hall. There was a good deal of highly polished brass about the front door too, smearless and promisingly hygienic. Here we paused for breath after the rickety ride which the chair had taken better than the passenger. Above the door there was a fanlight. The legend *Fortis Fortuna Adiuvat* stood out in a stained glass field of iris: one yellow, one blue, one white, rising from their own green leaves. It was a design after William Morris – perhaps long after William Morris. On either side of the door there were narrow panels of white frosted glass, covered with boldly etched acanthus. Not really related to the iris lilies, but pleasing in their own right.

The hall seemed very long. It was divided length-ways into three by an intensely floral carpet, bordered on either side by highly polished linoleum in a brown, yellow and green geometrical pattern in opposition to the carpet. Four square wooden tables squatted against the wall on either side. Each held a well burnished brass bowl with a lavish arrangement of gingernut – and camel-coloured dried grasses, bul-rushes and reeds, and in the dead centre what might have been the ghost of a sunflower. These arrange-ments were repeated with a precision that made you feel as though you were looking in a mirror that gave back not one, but four images of the same thing.

Half way down the hall there was a much newer wheel-chair. It seemed to be heavily armoured. I'd never seen a strait-jacket – but it made me wonder ... Four big rooms on either side were wide open as we passed. They seemed full of people wrapped in rugs and shawls, crouched in easy-chairs like crustaceans. Although the day was mildly sunny, all sat with their backs to the row of long, tightly closed windows in every room. All had blank faces turned towards the hall, as if they watched for visitors who never came. No smile answered mine, as we passed slowly by.

The big, round wall clock at the end of the main hall said that the afternoon was more than half over. Here we crossed a small passage into a kind of alley that ran down to the back door, three or four yards away. Where these passages met, in half light, we turned sharply left into my room. Someone switched the light on to dead white walls. The window was covered with the gathered folds of a nylon curtain which may once have matched the walls, but now was smoke-dyed grey. Helen held it aside and opened the window. Outside there was a good deal of smoke and a strong smell of something unpleasant burning. The kind, care-worn sister who had come to help me into bed said it was only the nearby incinerator.

Almost covering the wall at the foot of the bed was a double wardrobe, twice too big for the room. It had been heavily mistreated with a flat black stain and loomed within a couple of feet of the ceiling. The floor was covered with a sallow, mottled linoleum that shone as if it had been lacquered. Against the wall opposite the window, there was a squat, treacle-coloured chest with three good, deep drawers, and beside the bed, a table that might once have supported an aspidistra. It barely held a spindly metal lamp, a plastic water bottle and a glass. Not an inch of room for a book, or my companionable little bedroom clock that goes with me everywhere. In the corner nearest my bed was a shabby, dark brown armchair, the size and shape they used to have in the smoke rooms of old country pubs. It looked as if it had been heavily sat on by several generations of broad buttocks. A brass spittoon was the only thing needed to complete this setting.

Helen and I looked at each other. 'There wasn't another single room vacant *anywhere,* for a long-term patient,' she said.

Winter was still a month away, but the room, though airless, was cold. High above the door there was a small heatstrip, visibly in need of repair. After some hesitation, they decided to let me have my electric blanket from home. Sister apologized for the state of the heatstrip. She seemed to be the whipping-boy for the matron or manager, or whoever else ruled this fully registered, and by no means inexpensive, little private hospital.

A lively clatter opposite my door must have come from what would have to be the kitchen. Once more, Helen unpacked my bits and pieces and deftly stowed them away. We both produced a smile. Then she left me, promising to come back tomorrow with my blanket. High above the foot of the bed, an electric light dangled from an absurdly short cord. A shallow white plastic saucer made no pretence of shading the globe that glared at me with a cold eye. No use whatever for reading. The bedside lamp was as subdued as a night light. But Helen would deal with that.

Night came early to Haddon. Eerie calls and cries of protest, then loud and frequent instructions from hostile inmates, who must surely have been stone deaf, were met with patient exhortations. After about an hour, suddenly the battle ended. All seemed to have been sedated and bedded down. But this was no easy peace. A bell rang. A dozen others joined in chorus. Various demands were trumpeted over and over.

Later, the light outside my door went out. Then silence – at last. It was music – after what had gone before. Sometimes laughter rippled from what seemed to be a kitchen annexe across the passage. It was brightly lit and looked as though it was a servery and diningroom, and a staff room where the nursing-aides watched one of their portable T.V. sets.

An hour earlier than usual, Sister brought me five tablets and a cup of boiling water. I crumbled a chicken stock cube – provided by Helen – into it for my routine night cap. It was much too early for sleep.

Helen had left a paperback on my bed. There was nowhere else to put it. But tonight that cunning baggage, Lizzie Eustace, and the Eustace diamonds were simply not my dish. Besides, it was too cold to read. No star, not a hint of moonlight showed through the wide open window. Waves of darkness rolled over me, and in them were those expressionless, heavy-lidded faces of the afternoon. And that motto *Fortis Fortuna Adiuvat* twined among the flaglilies. 'The Brave'. Yes, indeed. That means you.

Perhaps an adoring husband had built this crumbling, old mansion for his young bride in the golden eighties. Young they must both have been to have chosen that motto. And its original name would have been much more flowery than Haddon. Those big front rooms with all the long windows, ready to flood with sun and fresh air, must once have been drawingroom, diningroom, bedroom, morningroom – probably not library or study. But all would have had lush Victorian wallpapers. The diningroom – red of course, covered with heavy gold scrolls. A clock, probably gilt, and under a glass shade, stands on the mantelpiece with its back to the vast mirror in a gilt frame. Nearby, on the massive sideboard, there's a bowl of cleverly contrived wax, or maybe coloured marble fruit. Not a mile away, fresh peaches and apricots can be had in abundance, and grapes as well. But Mama, whatever the season, *always* has a bowl of wax fruit on the sideboard. And the drawingroom – there the sunlit walls must have flowered in pink and yellow roses. Many small tables – holding a Dresden china shoe, and little flowery china boxes. There must be a rosewood whatnot, photographs, and still more photographs in glinting silver frames – Tom in uniform, Ursula with an ankle length skirt and a tennis racquet. Of course there would be a piano, probably an upright grand, with its fully exposed back draped in the rainbow silk Roger brought her back from India – as well as the gold mounted ivory tusk and the moonstone necklace ... Yes – this must be how it was. As for the bedroom – a moiré paper with silver stripes between knots of blue ribbon and rosebuds... Was she pretty and charming? He would have thought so. But their ghosts will never come hand in hand, haunting these rooms and that ragged garden. No, Haddon is not a place for young lovers... and so to sleep...

The friendly clop-clop of a horse stops at a word of earthy endearment. A snatch of song in a fruity baritone, and the milkman runs up the steps to the back door, with at least a crate of milk bottles jangling. But no crash. Four a.m. Not light yet. Day has already begun. If you are bedded down with the birds it may be that a biological clock tends to wake you with the birds – if not before.

Almost daylight. The hall has become a noisy thoroughfare. A nurse drags a heavy, acrid-smelling bag past my door, down the steps and probably into the laundry which seems to be under the spread of iron roof a few steps from my window.

Breakfast – no comment.

Meg, fresh, slim and friendly, comes to 'do' my
room. It will be her pride to keep it spotless, I can see.
She is already grandmother to three, she tells me.
Surely she must have gone from kindergarten to be
churched? But no. She was seventeen, she says with a
very faint Scots burr. One daughter married. There's
husband, two sons, and a very old father-in-law at
home to be cared for, too. She works from seven till
midday at Haddon. Her marketing is done on the
way home – all of which sounds to be a rather fine
performance. But she tosses it off lightly.

More of those eldritch noises – and not very far
away. Already I'm beginning to think of these others
as an impersonal 'They'. I'm the castaway – and the
name of my desert island is Haddon. Like the grave, it
is a very private place.

Sunday No visitors today. Not many will come
more than once. It is not simply that it is cold and
comfortless. There's something aggressive about the
room, even when you are used to it. A few, like
Amanda and Rose, can make their own good
weather, wherever they are. But only a few.

Because there is so little coming and going from
outside, and no communication worth mentioning
inside, living in a nursing home is an odd kind of
segregation. It's like being lost in a fog that closes
down more heavily, just as you think you can see
your way out.

Bed as a residence is not a thing to cultivate. To
wake at an acceptable hour, stretch your body, spring
out of bed and draw in the breath of early morning
from the garden – to spend the day among *people*,
with not too much work and a little play – then go
comfortably tired to bed: *that* is different. This bed I
would like better if the mattress did not yield to me as

easily. It sags with every movement, so that it seems that one day it must surely wrap itself completely around me.

There are only a few feet between my door and the kitchen. Not always unpleasantly, the clatter of real life drifts over me, from breakfast time till mid-afternoon. At least every second day this little world is shattered by a crash of china. On my tray, this same china looks quite thick enough to withstand anything... On weekdays, there is a cook who talks non-stop, never waiting for an answer. Her voice booms, as if it comes from the depths of a cave.

There's a hint of sun today in my small wedge of sky, but it does not touch my room. The sense of segregation is so palpable, you feel as if at any moment you will be tightly enclosed in a cocoon of isolation. Except for the milkman, before dawn, there's no sound of traffic passing by. Everything is negative. You never hear young people singing, speeding recklessly home from late parties, or even the stereophonic calls of philandering tomcats. Never the sound of children's voices, laughing and calling to each other as they race down the street. Only spasmodic screeching a few doors away, that would send cold shivers down anyone's spine. Yet they tell me nobody here ever has severe pain. It's like living in space. But it has its own grim kind of perm-anence, for we are all here for the term of our unnat-ural lives. Unless you are 'away with the fairies', the lasting anguish of being uprooted from your own kind must destroy you. And there's no speaking of it to anyone. Not to Helen – above all. Never to Helen.

Tuesday A writer, whose beautifully perceptive essays and letters are cherished by people lucky enough to own them, once asked me if I kept a diary.

My answer was 'No'.

'Begin today,' she said in her clipped, clear voice. Often I've wished I had taken her advice long ago. A diary cannot blush. It will let you unwind – without audible comment. My present safety valve is this rather scruffy, well-used notebook complete with ballpoint pen. If you must search your heart, better to put in your time writing of what you find there, than wasting your days wallowing in wretchedness.

There are twenty-nine patients at Haddon and one shower recess. Both shower and recess are shabby and in need of repair. In the small enclosure, adjoining the unscreened shower, are two toilets. These are semi-enclosed, with half doors, like they have in stables. The National Trust might care to set its seal on these, and on the plumbing as well. Few of my fellow-travellers are toilet trained. Or they've forgotten the rudiments, poor dears.

You may be ambulant, continent and intelligent, but you do not shower yourself. Fair enough. With loose tiles and a damaged spray, there may well be a risk of accident for the unwary. Besides, with only one shower, there has to be a pretty tight schedule. A sister escorts you from your bed, in a very clever chair with a seat exactly like a lifebelt. Sitting in this minus night attire of course, you are wheeled into the shower recess, and speedily soaped, rinsed and dried.

Going to the shower or toilet is the one way you are likely to meet any of your neighbours face to face. This is our village street and forum. Here they introduced me to Miss Wray. She likes to be called Violet. It is not her name. When she can be persuaded to walk she goes in big, very fluffy, pink slippers with gown to match. Above a fixed, bewildered smile she has masses of iron grey hair, with a very insistent purple rinse, so stiffly waved that it sits on her head just like one of the late Queen Mary's toques.

Sometimes the shower routine gives me the chance to exchange a thought or two with Sister Tyrone. Sister is book hungry and something of a collector. She has brought me two of her special treasures – McLorin's *Post Mortem* and *Mere Mortals,* long out of print. Hers are first editions. I've wanted to re-read them for years. We could have an exciting traffic of ideas, and a laugh or two, if only she had time. But except for Sister MacHeath and Nursing-aide O'Maire, no member of staff is here for more than three shifts a week – some for only one.

Friday This afternoon, in watery sunshine, five of us are wheeled out on to the grass and grouped in a tight half circle immediately opposite the front door. One is blind. Three are deaf, with modern hearing-aids, which they carefully keep out of action. All but one are unsmiling and completely withdrawn. My attempts at communication meet no response. Pity, and a sense of complete frustration wrack me. They have put me next to Miss Alice, with neatly coiled white hair and forget-me-not blue eyes. Sister says she is the last remnant of one of the very old pioneer families. She smiles at me. Perhaps she lip-reads a little. The sky has quickly clouded over. She looks up, smiles and says, 'The good Lord Jesus sends us the weather.' She repeats this phrase every few moments. Of them all, she alone seems to live happily in some unseen world of her own. She might even manage a simple jigsaw puzzle, or enjoy watching T.V. if there were room, or any opportunity for it. All the others stare, hard-eyed, into space. Well rugged-up as we are, within half an hour it is considered too cold to linger, and all five are soon wheeled inside again. Frankly, I don't think a good time has been had by anyone, though I would have been glad to stay in the fresh air for a while with only a book for company. The tragedy of this sad assortment at Haddon is that almost everyone has ceased to be a person. Nothing seems to touch the emptiness of lives so far astray from even the fringe of ordinary human values. If only one could do something about it. There's something so cold about mere passive acceptance. Probably the life-cycle of a flying beetle holds more interest and companionship than do the lives of the twenty-nine patients under this roof.

But there is one grand exception, Sister Tyrone tells me. She is known to the staff as 'The Admiral' – a tall, bony woman with a voice like a trombone. They say she treats the ward as her quarter-deck. She it is who orders the light put on and off, according to her fancy. There's no bowing to reason with her. She insists on the heating being up or down, and has a special place reserved for her chair, which no one else ever dares to claim. No loss of individuality about 'The Admiral'. And such is her commanding presence that her orders are invariably carried out, they tell me.

Lately, someone has produced a learned thesis on 'The Social Behaviour of Pigs'. It makes me wonder if anyone has thought of making a study of confused and forgotten, antisocial old ladies in nursing homes.

Helen says forget all this. Helen, to forget about it, in your surroundings, would be no problem. How can one believe that these human beings, who often live well into their eighties, could not at some stage have been shown a way of finding in the smallest activity an awareness and a reason for living, instead of spending long days staring into space? Except for the very few, there must be a time, before the point of no return, when they can be helped to keep their footing in the reality of here and now.

Monday The sun being high enough over the yard-arm, Sister is about to pour me a brandy. Suddenly, without a word, she abandons glass and bottle and darts from the room. Minutes later she is back with apologies. 'The emergency bell in the toilet,' she gasps. 'I had to run. Miss Montmorency wished to make a serious complaint.' Sister is a good mimic. She now speaks with an air of freezing dignity:

'Sister, there is not a knife and fork in here.'

'But, Miss Montmorency, we don't have knives and forks in the toilets.' 'Indeed,' says Miss Montmorency, seated in lavatorial splendour, 'then there should most certainly be a spoon and fork here.' Sister laughs. If she didn't, she would weep.

Tuesday Last night a volley of hailstones battered the long iron roof outside my window. Its length and strength were like the rattle of machine guns in one of those no-horror-spared war films. This morning's paper says it's the heaviest hailstorm Melbourne has had in over sixty years.

Five weeks have oozed away since my first day here. I miss the groups of nuns in their white habits that I used to see from my upstairs room in Prince Edward's, sailing along the tree-lined street to the Cathedral for early mass. When there is a breeze their veils fly behind like a wedge of wild white swans. Here you are solitary. Yet, sometimes a nursing-aide walks into my room for no imaginable reason, and departs without saying a word. It may be part of the routine of the place, but it makes me feel as over-exposed as a goldfish. Our life is what our *thoughts* make it. That's not my thinking. Marcus Aurelius said it nearly two thousand years ago. If he is right, much of my time here is spent living in sin.

This morning, for the first time, our matron called to see me. A big woman by no means unattractive to look at, in a brittle, well-groomed way. They tell me she never wears a uniform. This morning she was in rather opulent tweeds. The black olives Helen brings me seemed very much to her taste. Apart from them, she was in no way interested in me. Her immediate concern is plainly the store-room, on which she keeps a comprehensive hand. Mustard, for instance, might have made that grim, stark sausage, brought me, unaccompanied, for yesterday's evening meal, a little more palatable. To Sister MacHeath's painful embarrassment, the mustard is kept tightly locked away. And nowhere is that key to be found.

Matron stayed for quite a time. She talked a good deal about orchids – 'masses of them' – growing in her own private garden. She enlarged on her hair-dressing appointments, and her dealings with an exclusive little boutique.

The husband, who followed her into my room, was a neat, well-tailored little man. He manages Haddon. His manner suggests that he could be motivated by an inbuilt computer. They are indeed a very practical pair. Today from Amanda, some exquisite French perfume. It is in a flask about four inches high, crystal clear and patterned all over in a delicate tracery, like fine black lace. It is so perfectly made you almost feel the enchantment must vanish if it is ever opened.

Very late – Tonight, between six and seven, I hear heart-broken whimpering. It sounds so like a hurt

24

child, the thought is past bearing.

'Sister, there are no children here, are there?'

She hands me my nightly ration of pills, white, yellow, pink, beige and purple. A pause.

'No, that's Miss Agley, weeping because she doesn't want to have a shower. Don't worry, my dear. She's already had it. Now don't take those pills for at least a couple of hours, will you?' Then she is gone.

Tonight there will be a most unusual sister on duty. She is married and only works one night a week. Her vitality sends out sparks, and her humanity is bottomless. She has, as her permanent offsider, a nursing-aide, who, without any padding or make-up, and with just a touch of white to her hair, would be perfect for the nurse in *Romeo and Juliet*. She is a big, mothering hen whose feathers nothing can ruffle. Like me, she is garden-minded and loves cottage flowers – clove pinks and primroses and daffodils, and of course, campanulas, with a thought for rosemary, lavender and mint as well. If it is not too hectic a night, she will make time to curse the snails, and tell me how her garden grows, when she brings me my cup of boiling water. In this, I dissolve one of Helen's soup cubes by way of a night-cap, as usual.

Friday Helen to see me. She comes, bringing every comfort she can think of. But she need only bring herself. Which is everything. It's all very well to say 'no man is an island'. When man has no one to share a laugh with, a simple meal, or a glass of wine, no one to talk over a book, or a snippet of news with, he is indeed an island, and a ghost-infested one at that. Pain can be endured. But the laceration of one's spirit and senses in this place is quite another thing. Only a saint could bear this. A saint is what I'm not.

June

Monday⌀ June comes blustering in. The wind sounds as if it could blow the horns off a buffalo. It is a long time since I've seen a buffalo. *Query:* Have buffaloes horns? I have no way of finding out in here. It could be good weather to write, though, and scratch the hard surface of a long day. A pen in hand sometimes gives me an exquisite sense of well-being.

Thursday⌀ But Tuesday was, indeed, no place for a pen. Pain . . . The deadly heaviness that clamps you to the bed. Restlessness. And yet, a grim lethargy as well. Hurried, insistent short breaths, as if a tighter and tighter cord is knotted across your chest. The bell. *Ring the bell.* Rapid drumming below your left shoulder . . . At last the injection . . . It doesn't kill this clutching pain. But after a while, it begins to make you less mindful of it. Slowly, something, not quite sleep, but near enough to forgetfulness seeps through you. Then at last, you are set free.

Monday⌀ Today, in a questing frame of mind, I ask our very professional Sister Gareth when does one begin to be geriatric.

'Oh, at about forty-five,' she tells me.

So, old age with its diseases and alleged disabilities, begins at a time when most of the world's most gifted men and women have not yet done their great creative work. But Sister, Paganini long past sixty was still playing that Concerto of his, which they say has so many hazards that no concert violinist cared to tackle it until Menuhin came along. And Sybil Thorndike was still creating parts, in good company, at eighty. Discipline, and a fantastic memory were on her side, of course.

Yet Ninon de l'Enclos, that alluring, seventeenth century charmer, towards the end, confided to a friend that 'Old age is a woman's hell'. Just what would she have said of Haddon? And Ninon was by no means neglected. At eighty she still had lovers who came to enjoy her beauty and her wit. And more intimate favours as well, it is very reliably stated. Nearly all the great autobiographies have come from men well past forty-five – from Gibbon to Bertrand Russell, who was still writing, with humanity and sweet reason, forcefully enough to excite the younger generation when he was all of ninety.

And what about Michelangelo, Renoir, Picasso and Chagall? Or Verdi, Toscanini and Artur Rubinstein? Alfred Hitchcock, adventuring into his seventies, is still cinema's master of suspense – and Churchill, leader when there was no one younger with the heart to lead. If you think about it for a moment, it's plain that at eighty or so Tito is not doing too badly, either, keeping Jugoslavia out of reach of Big Brother, and out of economic strife, as well. No, Sister Gareth. No one can convince me that any age in itself is a disease, or quite ineffectual. Old age is a state of mind. And its ruthless enemy is convention, not the biological clock. Experience, maybe a long working life, and memory reaching back to a past crowded with men, women and events, are not often the stuff that apathy and disease feed on. Somewhere, environment and lack of occupation take over.

It's true enough that most of the old ladies at Haddon do turn vacant gazes to the world. A few of these faces have a strange look of warped innocence. And here and there you meet a glance of chilling malignity. Sometimes, one strays disturbingly into my room. Science is keeping them alive, but it isn't really on their side. If they had the smallest interest to keep their hands busy, like threading rainbows of beads to amuse retarded children, they might be less ready to deliver a well-aimed clout on the face, or buttocks, of a good-humoured, compassionate nurse. Who knows what a chartered bus-ride might do for those who are viable, an occasional visit from a social worker, or a regular session with an occupational therapist? Any small diversion gives a little meaning to life in a vacuum.

The forbidden thing should be to brand all elderly men and women as senile. Everyone who lives grows older. The majority don't grow soured, helpless, or bitter and irresponsible, simply because the passing years slow down their tempo of living. One of my favourite visitors, well past her eightieth birthday, gets her car out and drives herself and a sister over to see me every ten days or so. And there's no special calendar to measure the time or capacity to think, or to feel. Exquisite singing, or a violin or oboe superbly played can send sensuous shivers of delight down an elderly spine. Besides, people do fall passionately in love at seventy, when 'with-my-body-I-thee-worship' still means precisely what it says.

Wednesday⫻ Amanda has lent me Enid Bagnold's rather dashing autobiography. On her own reckoning E.B. was past eighty when she finished it. A full life, happiness and success give her plenty to say, and she says it all with surpassing candour, warmth and humour. A witty, delightful patchwork of a book. It is kind and clever of Amanda to send it as an antidote to living here, where everything is low-key, except the shrill, mindless ramblings of some lost soul staggering on the way to freedom without end.

Thursday⚓ There can't be many places better equipped than Haddon for you to graduate in loneliness and rejection. The days are long, and though the staff are friendly they simply haven't time to talk. Perhaps this sense of being a castaway comes from being indefinitely confined to this kind of room. Oh to walk to the gate and collect a letter from the box, or perhaps have a word with a passer-by.

Friday⚓ Still turning things as they are inside out, and trying to think of ways to renovate them. Pity, sermons, weeping and revulsion are not enough. Someone must tell the truth about this world of mist and fog. The wonder is that there are enough people to stay alive for four, five or ten years in such places. Not only are they always full, most of them have incredibly long waiting lists, as well. There must be something, inbuilt, that keeps people alive for all these years with nothing but bare walls to gaze at, and nothing to hope for. 'The Admiral' seems to be clearing the decks for action. Since early morning there have been sounds of considerable strife. It can't be civilized to uproot reasonably intelligent, ambulant old men and women from the well-worn, loved surroundings of a lifetime, and divorce them from their cat or dog. They miss that little brown teapot, in the red woollen cosy Florence made. Even if you can no longer dig your garden it must still be happiness to sit by your window and see how the pansies and petunias a neighbour has planted for you are growing. Better still, to sit on your verandah and watch the world pass by. They have few needs that can't be met by Meals-on-wheels, a call from one of those warm, outgoing visiting nurses – and one friend to look in, from time to time. In China 'old man' and 'old woman' are still terms of endearment. A benevolent government might even be moved to provide a free telephone service for elderly men and women needing a little care. It would be far less costly than subsidizing years of the traumatic experience of living in most geriatric nursing homes. For there seems to be a long way to go before an honest distinction between treatment of those who are geriatric, and those who are mentally ill, is recognized by these little hospitals.

For the evening meal at four o'clock, cottage pie. A homely alias for a few hard, brown little berries of meat, floating around in watery gravy. All is lightly masked in a transparent veil of mashed potato. This can be followed by nursery pudding, covered in custard, and perhaps cream, and a glass of milk. But not for me. I'm allergic to all the good things the friendly cow provides. But an occasional poached egg, or a grilled lamb cutlet, or egg and bacon would be quite a banquet, without any trimmings at all.

Monday Ianthe came today, the hard way, bless her. Three trains, with waits between, and then a walk. For a short time in her youth, she toured with an English Shakespearean company and is still to be remembered as one of Lear's ruthless daughters. Her affair with the theatre lives on in the way she walks, in her poise, and in the way she uses her lovely, musical voice. Today, by special request, she read me two of Shakespeare's *Sonnets*, as I've never heard them spoken, except by John Gielgud. I know people who seem to delight in taking a scalpel, or X-ray to poetry. It's my delight just to listen with every pore, and live with it, till the echoes die. The *Sonnets* have much the same effect on me as the Flower Song from

Carmen used to have on my ninety-year-old gran. She was a very pretty old woman, and whenever she heard it she would light up. Her cheeks could flush like a girl's, especially if someone played that very lush record of Caruso's or Martinelli's for her. She never told us why. Ianthe's visits are a joy. The beautiful sounding of words, a child's laughter, bird's song – these are some of the longings that plague me in this tight room.

Wednesday⫝̸ My lamp is burning into the early hours of tomorrow. Sister looks in. 'Still awake – and *writing*, at this time of the night? You should be asleep. It's not quite three yet. Would you like another of your tablets?' I nod. Soon she brings me the tablet, and with it a comfortable cup of tea. It's weighty, and as I sip, I think of the frail blue Copenhagen cup and saucer at home, that the children gave me. Sister is good. She shakes up my pillows and makes them as comfortable as her tea. But sleep does shun me.

What kind of dreams clamour for a hearing in these rooms all round me? Too many ideas chase each other through my mind. Prancing up and down and round and round, but always ending in the same place, like the painted horses on merry-go-rounds, when Helen and I were children.

Sleep should be earned by work, or else by some kind of activity that has an end in view. There's no plot to unravel in the little dramas that are set to end inside these walls. All the players have to do is sit and wait for death to make one of his not infrequent entrances.

Friday⫝̸ Shortages of staff, and very few expert at that, call for the less predictable patients to be bedded down by five in the afternoon. Peace takes over, for a while. Heavily sedated, in half an hour they are dead to the world. Without this routine, probably few of the younger nursing-aides could last very long. But small wonder that a clutch of old ladies is already awake, and clamouring to be up and dressed at 3 a.m. It has been a night of alarms and excursions. But this sounds like a riot. Even when they are up they can't or won't read, Sister tells me, and seldom say a word to each other. If only they had something, however trivial, to give their lives some meaning, and fill the long sameness of the days.

There's a street of small cottages, not far from our home, and in one of them lives a colourful old character known to everyone as Aunt Maudie. She loves to plant marigolds and lobelias in her tea-tray sized front garden, and she's not above pulling these up, from time to time, to see if they are growing. On occasion, she may playfully turn the hose she has been given on a passer-by. But everyone likes Aunt Maudie. She lives alone, and she's happy. She has her reasons for living. Among them is her big, sleek black cat, Finnegan, who, according to rumour, lives exceedingly well.

Even at Haddon there are two or three that might be made happy for a while with a little plot of earth, a bundle of seedlings and a trowel and a small corner of this big, sad garden. Judging by the volume of sound they can produce, they seem strong enough for this exercise, and they might enjoy the spice of a little competition.

Tonight, I believe I could sleep if I could hear the gentle swish of the wind through pine trees, or the sleepy ebb and flow of the sea. Even a plant will die in a cell without sun, with never a breeze blowing through the wide open window.

Monday☞ Yes, *Blue* Monday. Nothing in this world will make me used to that insinuating, acrid smell of urine-soaked bedding. This morning it is draped again on tottering, cane chairs, and along the railing of the verandah that runs with the wall that holds my only window. If it is closed, the room will be airless. It's all very well for Helen to say forget it. The human body will not be ignored. When smells and sights and sounds flay the senses, it retaliates in all kinds of devious ways. That window and the door must both be kept open, however cold it is, to give me my issue of oxygen.

Thursday☞ A morning the colour of ashes. The heat-strip is mended, at last. The light shows, but so modestly that Helen says it doesn't make itself felt. She puts her bunch of winter roses where I can see them – miracles in pale green and heliotrope. Cold as it is, Sister Mead comes, too, just as she promised, with some exquisite pink camellias from the family garden. If one could only borrow some of the gay hardihood of these flowering things.

Perhaps there will be some Mozart on the air tonight. And I will look at all my carefully saved cards of wonderful reproductions of the Post-Impressionists and their heirs, that Amanda sends me. I remember years ago, Mao Tse-tung told his people: 'The arts are not flowers to be added to a piece of embroidery but fuel for a person in snowy weather'.

July

Friday☞ And so to July, and a meeting with Miss Call-Me-Violet, on the way to the shower. All she wants in this world, it seems, is a diamond ring. She tells me she is going abroad on Wednesday. Always on Wednesday. Sister says this yearning for a diamond ring never leaves her. Then *why,* oh why doesn't someone go to Woolworth's and buy her a diamond ring?

The trip abroad is pure fiction. Whatever else there is in her clouded mind to come and go, the ring is always there. She must have a story. Once, long ago, when she was young, and probably quite pretty, was she, perhaps, governess or lady-companion, and did the son of the house fall in love with her? Perhaps he gave her a diamond ring. Which was afterwards taken back. Or, he may have promised her a plain gold ring, and neglected to do anything more about it. Until it was too late. Whatever is past hasn't carved a single line on her chubby face. Yet, whenever we meet she has a look of bitter-sweet bewilderment. As if she is trying to put together a jigsaw puzzle that will never work out because her diamond ring is the piece that is missing.

The sisters say they come to love these Miss Violets. They care for them, sometimes in the midst of ingenious provocation, with the patient, humorous gentleness that people usually keep for small children. But what betrayals, quarrels, loneliness, and rejection must bring so many of these unloved shadows here.

Sunday Although Helen stays me, week by week, with grapefruit, soup cubes, oranges, brandy, liver pâté, and delicious black olives, I'm often hungry. Weight is pouring off Helen as she shuttles here from home so often. The frustrating truth is that I'm putting on weight, and losing energy to the point where getting in and out of bed is a kind of athletic feat.

34

Friday⫶ Our menu is rigidly carbohydrate. Good, no doubt, from the economic standpoint. And for some of us, cereals, milk puddings with custard, sometimes cream, and milk drinks, every day, may be adequate, but not exactly ideal fare. But if you have a heart problem and severe anaemia, and are allergic to milk, whether it's plain, or in fancy dress, there must be days when you and hunger are in no way strangers. My impossible dream is a poached egg, bacon and a little grilled chop, or a simple baked apple, not tinned fruit that appears after long intervals, and then day after day, until the tin at last is empty.

Wednesday⫶ Angina again. But the night sister and nurse are superb. One on either side, they lift me up, as gently as if I were a new-born child, then stack more and more pillows at my back, to make breathing easier. Sister throws up the window, as high as it will go, and pins back the curtain to let in more air. Then she leaves me with Nurse, and takes off for the injection that brings rest, and forgetfulness of pain. She is so quick, and calm, and good.

Friday⫶ Enter Rose, vibrant and unexpected, well after visiting hours, as usual. But it is good to see her, whenever she comes.

'Could you drink a glass of champagne?' she says. *'Could I?'*

'No, don't open it now. Have it for your supper. I've brought some oysters to go with it.'

Generous Rose. She is always involved in something. This time it is arranging hospitality for players in the famous symphony orchestra that is coming from the other side of the world to give concerts in Melbourne shortly. Yet, in the midst of the three-ringed circus kind of life she revels in, she so often finds time to do the kindest thing at a bedevilled moment. Today, Rose is the exotic touch these cold walls need, in a dramatic, brown tweed cape over a slack-suit to match. 'Not new,' she says – bought last time she was in Paris. New or old, for me it is Paris come to life. Rose leaves me with the warming touch of another world.

Then, I ring my bell and invite Sister to open that beckoning, be-ribboned bottle. She brings it back with thin brown bread and butter, wedges of lemon, and the oysters, all provided by Rose, quite sure that such trimmings would not be found here. Sister will not join me in a glass as she is on duty. So empty as I am, I down that small bottle of champagne, watching the minute stars that jet to its pale-gold surface.

Tuesday That loathsome, acrid, wet bedding draped outside my window again this morning. Something I'll never learn to take. Strangely enough, this never happens when my nice young G.P., grown more perceptive these last few months, comes to visit me.

Sister Tyrone is on duty today. She shines above this murky pool.

Thursday Another white night. In desperation, a usually most forbearing night sister shouts at a stone-deaf old lady who rowdily insists on being up and dressed at 3 a.m. She screams back, with incredible volume, in the raucous, toneless voice of the long-time deaf. After all this, I'm as wide awake as she is, lying in the dark, thinking what an experience it would be to see a star in that slit of sky outside my window.

Friday These four white walls, stark as bleached bones, are closing in on me. The management refuses to let me have two small angle-pins to hold a couple of prints. Perhaps they have their reasons. Only walls as thin as cardboard could let in sounds the way these do. Well, think of something else to give a spot of warmth and colour to these ghastly spaces. Small shelves to hold a few books? After all, they can only – and probably will – say a curt 'No.'

Monday Rain. Rain. Few visitors. But always Helen. And often Kate and Sybil. All find it unspeakably cold here. That reluctant strip-heater is an essay in public relations. No one can feel it. Perhaps it is just there to give an impression of winter cheer.

My need for familiar things grows with these endless days. It would be comfortable to have Shakespeare beside me, to sip and savour. And my *Concise Oxford Dictionary,* too. There's a deal of easy, satisfying adventure to be had as you riffle the pages of a good dictionary, pecking at curious phrases and discovering lively words you've never met before.

Helen often says how much possessions mean to me, and that they mean nothing to her. Perhaps this may be because she has so many. Yet, in a way she's right. Helen would never take kindly to tyranny – and least of all, to the tyranny of things. But I have no delight in merely owning. My little worktable is not just a treasured antique in beautifully inlaid walnut. It is something that four generations of us have used. I've lived with it for the best part of my life, and love it. The old silver and Venetian point, that are kept for birthdays and other family celebrations, affect me in much the same way. They are not mine. They belong absolutely to Helen. But for me, they are filled with remembrance of the best of days past – Christmas and birthdays, with the family dozen, of various shapes and sizes, all clustered round the solid, old cedar table. Everyone laughing, everyone talking in that happy 'Do-you-remember-when?' voice.

And the Christmas tree. Always very seriously decorated with a star, tinsel, and baubles by the youngest who hang their gifts from its branches. Then, after they are very reluctantly persuaded to go home, we bring out our carefully hidden surprises for them, and pile them around the tree.

When you're no longer part of all this, the garland of faces round an old table, decked with flowers and bon-bons, lit up with crystal and silver, becomes a very intimate remembrance of things past.

The way to learn about segregation is to live with it. Very soon you know that the complete human being that you still hope you are, is slowly beginning to perish. Memory is your only light.

Tuesday If Haddon has a soul it must be Sister MacHeath. Next month she goes on long leave. She's tall and spare, and must be sixty. Her vitality is staggering, but it is her depths of selflessness that make you believe in miracles. She was born on a farm in the West. For years she worked, for a just visible wage, as trained nurse, emergency doctor, philosopher, and friend to the people in the Far North. Sometimes she travelled to her patients on horseback, with the barest amount of equipment, sometimes in a rickety old Ford. I've pieced this together from our brief encounters when, in her own special way, she has been caring for me, body and soul.

Wednesday This morning on shower parade, I meet Mrs Thatcher. She always makes me think of the elegant phrase with which I once had to fill a whole page of my copy-book: 'When Gentlefolk meet, Compliments are exchanged.' She is very erect but walks with a cane, steadily, like a dowager in a costume play, and never wears glasses, though she knits or crochets all day long, for children's charities. Whenever we part, she gives me a tender little pat and a peck on the cheek, as if I were a young daughter. She is ninety-two, and looks as fresh as a flower. Hers is a gently spoken, very lovely old age, and even in these surroundings, has charming dignity.

Friday 'Change beyond report, thought, or belief.' The aspidistra stand is gone. My own bedside table takes its place. This holds water, lamp and book, a bowl of fruit and my small, companionable clock. It has three drawers. One will serve as dressing-table, the next as desk, and the last for thimble, scissors, needles and thread. The snippets of blue, violet, aqua, the pink that Gaugin loved to paint, and some sunflower yellow, powdered with white daisies that Veronica has brought for my patchwork, will go in as well. My little Victorian rockingchair, covered with the faded gold velvet that goes so well with cedar, is in the corner, instead of the tatty brown leather monster. And not only that – a set of shelves, some eigthteen inches wide, will hold a few books, and still leave room for Madame Renoir in her dark gown, with her flowery red hat, and her enchanting small daughter. Helen has given me this amazing reproduction, which at a glance looks just like an oil-painting. There is room for my print of Cézanne's *Blue Iris,* too. Later, Sister comes to view the new interior. No comment – just a smile. But it convinces me that, aided and abetted by Helen, she has engineered all this before she takes off for Singapore and places East.

Saturday The mere sight of it makes me happy. But the company of my nephew, David, who on his midterm week-end from boarding-school, comes to arrange table, chair and shelves for me to get the easiest view of them, adds another hue to my rainbow.

Sunday ♫ Sister Ariel makes her entrance. In the front door, and down the hall, she sings pseudo-opera at the top of her voice. Then into my room, ballet, with elaborate arm movements to suggest *Swan Lake* – also pseudo. She's slim and very light of foot. And she must have lost weight, for in her slightly too big, crisp white uniform, as she bows to my applause centre, right and left, she looks like a top-heavy cloud. This entertainment, all for my benefit, happens on Saturdays and Sundays. There is a reason. She tells me she has a husband who spends all his week-ends golfing, dining, dancing – and whatnot – with Another Lady. Ariel, which is in fact not her name, is a good nurse, and would be an even better companion, if only this were part of Haddon's therapy. It seems she is perpetuating the myth of a happy family until their only child, now a final year student, graduates.

The feeling that she is badly needed here, I think, gives her a kind of second-hand happiness. Besides, by going out every Saturday and Sunday, she lets friends and neighbours know that she, too, has a permanent week-end engagement. She never changes into uniform until she is here. By this slight fiction, she remains self-honoured, though maybe not secure.

No visitors today. Nothing marks the passing of the years for me as indelibly as the dwindling of the troop of friends who call me by my given name. But I'm no longer aunt to my nieces and nephews, and a good many of their friends. They, too, are beginning to use my first name, which charms and touches me a little, too.

The coppery bronze and russet leaves Rose brought from Macedon have a lovely nostalgic autumn tang. It is saddening to think how much more beautiful the dying leaf can be than the slow decay of human beings under this very roof. My transistor is sometimes temperamental, but tonight it brings me the lilting of de Falla's *Seven Popular Spanish Songs*. They are sung by Victoria de los Angeles – all their lovely colour matched by the warmth and ripeness of her exquisite singing. If only this sound could linger, the room would never again be quite sunless.

Monday☞ Those songs of de Falla's are still with me, long after they are heard no more. Whatever else I've lost, the joys of the senses are still for me – and me for them. On days when I feel like a fish that will never get back to the sea, a favourite air of Bach's or Mozart's will do more for me, music – but *Music* is the superb tranquillizer.

Wednesday☞ For the third or fourth time Miss Brinsway, a new patient, glides into my room, without so much as a knock on the door. Her eyes have those heavy lids that droop like a camel's. There is a notice on my door that says 'NO VISITORS PLEASE'.

'Why does that notice on your door say "NO VISITORS"?' she enquires in a tone as bitter as alum.

'Because I'm not well enough to have visitors,' is my soft, but maybe testy answer. She stays on, determined to let me enjoy her company.

Round and round the room she glides, touching all my bits and pieces on the way. She is a compact little body, pallid, except for her strangely glinting eyes, tightly set dark hair, and her bright peacock-blue suit. Had she, by chance, seen my rockingchair, table and shelves being brought in on Friday and come to inspect them? As she pelts me with questions, I get more and more breathless. I could ring for Sister to come and take her away. But something, which I hope is compassion, stops me.

Round she goes. Those hard grey eyes keep darting at me. Something makes me think of the cold glitter of a newly-sharpened carving knife.

Suddenly she turns and stares at me, and says:

'I had nothing whatever to do with my sister being taken away. Nothing whatever.' Then, suddenly, she leaves me. She seems horribly afraid that anyone here may be faring better than she is. She gives no sign of pleasure at anything she sees. Just repeats her inspection and cross-examination. I've always been rather like the boy in the fairy-tale who wanted to learn to shudder, but I think I could be just a little afraid of Miss Brinsway.

Thursday Sister MacHeath is perturbed about Miss B's visits which continue, in spite of the notice she herself has put on my door. I wish I could dial a telephone and call up some well-loved voice. After such long absence it would be like dabbling in magic. But there's only one phone here, and in that box called the office there's not a spare inch to take a switchboard for another line, even if my means could be stretched to provide it. Still, it would be a most comfortable thing to have. This kind of ordinary, everyday conquest of space means more to millions and millions of human beings than any landing on the moon. It's such a simple way of breaking down an overwhelming sense of isolation. They have no pills to give you for that.

I wonder how much medical science knows about the impact of segregation, in places like Haddon, on men and women, who need professional care, but are ambulant, continent and intelligent?

July is nearly over. The air is damp and heavy and my window stands wide open to catch any stray breeze. Not a glimpse of a single star, much less the setting sun, or moonlight, since April. It must be all that wiring and the row of iron-roofed excrescences close by, that keep nature so severely in her place. Being wide awake through the small hours is somehow more endurable with the moving moon and a star or two for company...

Saturday Sister tells me Miss Brinsway has gone. She seemed so unloved. But I certainly feel safer without her. She looked as if she could at any time translate her frustration into violence. Poor, sad Miss B.

This afternoon an exquisite bowl of azaleas, camellias, like small pink peonies, deeper toned cyclamen, and a bunch of violets tucked in beside them, has come, quite unexpectedly, from Eve. They are all rather formally set in moss. No arrangement is needed. The moss just has to be kept moist. A most delightful way for anyone to remember you.

Sunday Gazing at Eve's flowers this morning takes me back to a frosty early spring day at Nara, where we were staying years ago. In the park with the magically carved Temple of Kasunga No Miya, which is Nara's crowning glory – there were hundreds of small tame deer. We were told that every autumn their antlers were cut so that they couldn't hurt anyone. They looked as if they belonged to a fairy-tale. So did the very old woman who sold us biscuits which the deer nibbled daintily from our hands.

But nobody had told us about The Tree. Grafted, with a classic sense of design, on the one stock there were a wisteria, a cherry, camellias and, I think, azaleas and other flowering shrubs as well. It was too early for the wisteria, but all the others were in flower. Slips of white paper tied with different coloured silk threads to every flowerless twig intrigued us. Had they been put there – but this seemed most unlikely – to scare the birds away? No, we discovered later. Those wisps of paper held the vows and prayers of young girls who yearned for their true loves to offer marriage – parents of course permitting. Everything in the park that fresh, spring day held a lingering air of enchantment. It wouldn't have surprised me if the Firebird – in ballet shoes – had crossed our path, as we found our way back to our hotel.

Monday Regretfully, I've finished the last of Trollope's Palliser novels – all six of them, lent to me by Kate and Sybil who stay me with so many of the good things that come in paperbacks. Trollope loved a duke, or a thoroughbred. And what a touch he had for social satire – not sharp, like a polished razor, but the more penetrating kind, that leaves you with a thoughtful smile long after the book is back on the shelf.

August

Monday Tonight, a longing to see the moving moon, and a star or two, possesses me. Even a lighted window, or a street lamp to throw shadows of bough and leaf on a painted wall would be something. For those who are completely disorientated and withdrawn, one of the few compensations must be that whims like these don't nibble away at your peace of mind. But better a mind that's alive, even if it does browbeat that poor old ass, your body.

Last night, one room away from mine, there was a heart still beating, and lungs still taking their turn. Yet, however well that heart keeps on serving the body, the mind is already dead. There is no reason or compassion in such sad pretence. She is friendless and rejected. Existence, supported by drugs alone, is not life.

Tuesday Again this morning 'The Amputee' keeps pacing up and down on her crutches past my door. She is tall and amazingly vigorous, and looks about thirty, with her fair curling hair cropped like a small boy's. Her skirt is a good four inches above her poor stump. Not so much as a scrap of gauze covers the raw, almost bleeding flesh. One of the most compassionate sisters notices her and says to me, 'This display is quite unnecessary. The woman is a sheer exhibitionist – and a pill,' she adds as she fixes my pillows.

This is the third day this has happened. Each time she passes she looks through the door towards me, as if she is making sure that someone sees her. She wears that raw wound as if it were a decoration. It tears me to pieces. And yet the crutches, and that show of raw flesh might in some bizarre fashion be to her what my ballpoint and squiggle pad are to me.

Helen comes with fruit and brandy and the first daffodils. However grey the weather, daffodils always make my heart dance. They are like the sun in this room that is so dark that the baleful, one-eyed light on its skimpy cord is kept burning all day.

Thursday Sister Tyrone says sometimes she could do with a little revelry by night, though it seldom comes her way. Tonight is an exception. This affair is for the top brass, and for once, she's going. Gossip does not babble around Haddon, but I get the impression that her husband, and she loves him deeply, is a handsome weather-cock. The kind of air force and naval type who puts on *charisma* with his uniform.

Tonight, on her way to the mess, by special invitation, she calls to let me see how she looks in her 'gladrags'. The long frock with coat to match, are not new, but they make her sparkle with a new dimension. Out of uniform she looks smaller. At this moment she's a porcelain figurine, in jade and silver brocade. 'You'll have a proud husband, tonight, Sister.' 'You think so?' She raises an eyebrow, and gives me her quick, little smile. 'You really think so?' She's definitely amused. But she hasn't quite lost that first, fine careless rapture for him.

Saturday I have company, at last. Helen has brought me a portable T.V. set. It stands by my bed on a little table and rolls on castors that bring it in reach for tuning at the touch of a finger. Bed-bound, I've already walked those enchanting valleys of Nepal with masses of flowers on the way.

Monday Tonight, on T.V., Bertrand Russell talked about how and where the world is going. The occasion was his near ninetieth birthday. He spoke rather slowly, but with style – born, no doubt, of that old affair with his first love, Mathematics, where he says he found not only truth, but supreme beauty.

Helen is youthful and perceptive, and in no way claims possession because she has given life. Yet already one or two of her young, who should know better, are making her feel the generation gap. It's an ugly phenomenon in this permissive age which has so many attractive ways. We're leaving our world, stuffed with outworn creeds, for them to renovate. They have the drive and the courage to do it. But courage, even like theirs, isn't enough. Neither is the belief that if you have youth nothing else matters.

Since I was a talkative five-year-old I've been drawn to older people. At first, because they could usually tell the most enthralling stories. In my reckoning, there's no age-test for friendships. And I've never been aware that one age, in itself, is more repulsive than another. There are bores for all seasons. Helen, darling, you should remind your offspring that middle-age breathes exactly the same air, knows the same joys of desire and being desired, as your endearing young.

A new, transient nursing-aide on the evening shift. She's friendly. Attractive in an amusing, full-blown synthetic blonde way, and prepared to be entertaining. Her flawless well-shaped hands have had expert care. Her nails, the longest I've ever seen, are lacquered carmine. Can they be real? And her lipstick is, of course, incarnadine.

Watching me turn over small, many coloured hexagons for my patchwork she tells me she is making a patchwork quilt – by machine. 'But big. *Very* big. And psychedelic. If you know what I mean.' A lavish spread of arms shows me the size of her quilt that I can equate with nothing less than the Great Bed of Ware.

Nurse does not favour uniform. Her flared, black velvet skirt would pass for a tu-tu. Above it is something in challenging pink, elaborately and most expertly knitted – no doubt by those busy, fascinating hands. Even now, though on duty, they are at work on a maze of macramé.

She's friendly, but not quite real. How did she become a nursing-aide? She's a poster by Toulouse Lautrec.

Tuesday ♂ And wild and grey it is. No visitors will come to-day. My Pandora's Box offers (a) U.S. Variety series; (b) U.S. Drama serial; (c) U.S. Drama serial; (d) U.S. Cartoon series; (e) Children's sessions. I think I prefer a little Trollope.

Later – A cunning random twist of the dial brings me a sweep of open country, rolling gently towards the skyline. A girl and boy race by with a labrador. Child's laughter. No description. Just sound. Sometimes bird-song and when that is lost, background music with echoes of green pastures. No grazing land, and the Dividing Range not very far away. Bored, aristrocratic rams, fussed over by a maternal collie, are clotted round occasional gums and kurrajongs. We're on the road with a horseman galloping by. Now a flash of wings. The lens slides on to a sunlit pool. Wild duck fly over, upwards, towards puffs of cloud, clustered like four-o'clocks.

Less than half an hour, and I've been out and far, with a fair wind blowing. I wish I could say thankyou to that cameraman.

Still reading at 2 a.m. For over half an hour sounds of a drunken brawl have shattered the air. They seem to come from just outside my window. Weary and sleepless, I ring for Sister and ask if this brawling can possibly be stopped.

'It is not a brawl, Miss Newton. What you can hear is a patient in the ward at the end of the passage.'

Only one room away from me. I'm not convinced.

'It sounds like two people, Sister. One voice is harsh and deep, like a man's. She must be very strong, to have that powerful voice, Sister.'

But no. It seems she's a little old wisp of a woman.

'She must be in agony to cry out like this. Couldn't she have an injection to help her?'

48

'She's been given everything possible to relieve pain.' Sister is tired, too. 'As far as we can tell she's not in any pain whatever. Do try and go to sleep. I'll close your door.'

I try to read...And again...But nothing in this world will close my ears to those sounds. Now coarse, harsh, deep. Like a man's voice, fighting back. Then shrill, distraught, wailing. It could be man and woman wrestling with life and death.

I read the same page over and over again. It holds no meaning for me whatever. Nearly four o'clock. It won't be light for hours.

The deep, bass cries have stopped. Strange, falsetto wailing pierces the closed door. As if remorse for the seven deadly sins was tearing at her heart. It is stifling in here. I ring for someone to open the door.

Keening now, that rises and falls, rises and falls. A banshee wailing. And then thin, broken fluting like a lament for a heartless lost love.

Wednesday Seven o'clock. It is daylight, and my lamp still burning. Suddenly eerie silence takes over. You could hear a leaf fall on snow. Sister MacHeath comes on duty. She will have none of my open door.

'I'm closing your door, Miss Newton,' she says, coldly, as I've never heard her speak before. 'And see you keep it tightly closed.' Not one other word.

Outside the door a man is talking. A sound unlikely here, unless it is a doctor. And rarely, if ever, at breakfast-time. Silence. Even in the kitchen. A slow, male tread down the hall past my door. A pause. Then down the three steps that lead to the yard. The backgate clicks. Anguish ended. She is free.

Angina...No visitors today. I'm glad. This is no place for Helen. But late in the afternoon Sister MacHeath comes in and sits beside me. Easing back

her veil from her neat grey head, she says, 'This has
been a most *perplexing* day.'

'Perplexing?'

'Well, to begin with, late this morning dear old
Miss Buckley died, too. She had been with us for over
four years. She had such dignity.'

Just in time, I stop myself from asking her hasn't
Miss Buckley quietly fulfilled the intention that
brings every one of us to Haddon? But Sister loves
even these so often petulant, old women. She gives
them the patient gentleness that most people keep for
very young childen. She's tired, too.

Tomorrow, ten days later than she planned, she
leaves for her S.E. Asian holiday.

'Are you off duty, Sister?'

'Yes, off on the early plane tomorrow morning.
And I haven't packed a thing.'

'Then you go and find a glass. There's brandy here.
We'll have a quick one to speed you on your way.'
Which we do.

Thursday⧸ In the box of bits and pieces Helen
has brought here for me to dispose of, is *The Lady's
Casket*, by Miss Colman, 1849. Not by Annabel,
Belinda or Charlotte, but *Miss* Colman. Her book
measures about two and a half inches by three and is
bound in faded, dark blue linen with vanishing gold
curlicues on its spine. It is registered by*Mrs* Colman
in Massachusetts. Is Miss under twenty-one, perhaps?
Or is it thought unseemly for a young unmarried
lady to produce a book – perhaps almost as indelicate
as it would be for her to produce a baby? We shall
never know. But she fills her casket with quotations
from Addison to Xenophon. So she must have had
the run of a good library.

There's not one word by either of Miss Colman's

gifted countrymen, Nathaniel Hawthorne or Edgar Allan Poe, who were both writing in her time. It seems essential for an author to be dead to get into that casket. Besides, scarlet letters and croaking ravens may not have fitted too well in any lady's casket.

September

Tuesday Ten days since Sister MacHeath left us. It seems much longer. In this less than half-world there are phases when time seems to freeze. Twenty-four hours don't mark one day. They stretch into an uneasy eternity.

Today, half-asleep over a sedate morning paper. Held up in front of my eyes it is a screen, but not an entertainment. Suddenly someone is thrashing my legs and feet. I drop the paper and ring my bell as two tightly clenched fists descend on me again and again. And then I see her.

She is well above average height, big-boned but graceful as a young silver birch. Except for her pale gold hair, coiled on the crown of her head, she is blue from her chin to her slippers. She looks at me and the beating stops. It must be the blue that makes me see her as one of those goddess shapes on a Wedgwood urn. In clear-cut, unlined fairness she stands close to my bed. Pale as a statue and just as still, now that she has stopped flailing me.

I ring again. Efficient Sister Spencer arrives at last. She smiles when she hears my problem.

'This is Mrs Franklin-Smith, Miss Newton. My "baby" wouldn't hurt anyone.' Maybe. She has hurt my swollen feet and legs, considerably. Without a flicker of recognition, she lets Sister lead her gently away.

Wednesday Tonight, wide awake, long past comfort, yesterday's encounter haunts me. You don't ask questions at Haddon. But passions have been weaving. Never in my life before have I been bashed – in anger or in fun. It disturbs me to think that a stranger, aware in some twisted way of deep distress, must satisfy her frustration through another human being. And I feel that this has happened many times before to someone unable to escape from those clenched fists . . . A child? But such hate cannot be. An old song keeps echoing through my mind. 'Have you marked but the fall of the snow before the soil hath smutched it?' Though there is no blind to the window, except for a strip of light under the closed door opposite, darkness is opaque all around me. I don't think I can stay alive much longer in this cage of human beings.

Friday September is nearly over. A long, clanking chain of days. Few signs of spring. And not very much to look at on T.V. these days. Football, races, cartoons and pop music on the national station.

Wednesday Spring. It must be. Very early in the distance, I heard a bird's song. Faintly, and only once. And at breakfast-time there's a pigeon on the tin roof outside my window. I've never seen one there before. Soon he takes wing. Perhaps he's a carrier and was just resting in an arrow of sun.

Room-bound, I ask if there is any spot where I can sit for a while outside. No. Too cold. Being under-staffed they prefer their charges in easy reach. And that, without prejudice, means in bed.

Like most villas built in the seventies and eighties of last century, Haddon sends wide verandahs south and west to catch cool winds. A little shelter to the south could make them pleasant ways to take the air. That cypress hedge sets up a solid wall to the west about twenty feet high that no sun can penetrate. Very effective for cutting off sights and sounds within. But there's not one chink to let in sight or sound of the living world outside. Strangely, it doesn't give an atom of shelter to these wind-swept, but otherwise most desirable verandahs.

Thursday✍ Miss Graham is in the room next to me. Her only companion is a dignified old lady, usually asleep, sitting upright in her chair with a book on her lap, whenever I pass on the way to my shower. The room is half-dark, even with one small light burning all day. Miss Graham sits bolt upright, too, at a card table facing the wide open door. Sister Tyrone says Miss Graham wanted to join father and brother in the family profession. Her family for some reason rejected the mere thought of it. She was gifted with an unusual flair for design. It sounds like one of those families who consider a touch of genius not quite respectable. So she let herself be steered into teaching. 'So much more suitable for a woman, my dear,' says Sister Tyrone, darkly.

These showering episodes are much too brief. It is the one time and place where thoughts and observations can be unleashed with gusto – within that ten minute limit. And so now Miss Graham sits like a sphinx with wheat-coloured hair, day in and day out, at her card-table always opposite the wide open door, which she stares straight through, as she absently turns the pages of one glossy weekly after another.

What does she see? Nothing to do with living. But given pencils, watercolours and sketch-book she might from her cloudy threshold of awareness give form and colour to sights unseen by us – even find in her own private world some small tangible joy. Is the card-table a symbol for the drawing-table that might have given her life meaning?

For nearly half a year I've waved to her, almost every morning, passing. Today for the first time, a faint smile lights the mask that is her face. Like one candle on a child's birthday cake. For the first time she has flowers, too. Three daffodils in a glass close beside her on the table.

Friday☞ Helen again with letters, flowers and fruit. A dazzling card comes from Bangkok from Sister MacHeath. 'Midst pleasures and palaces – and sunlit ways, she would find time to remember me.

Saturday☞ Read from half-past two till nearly five this morning. Pitiful wailing again a couple of doors away. It is like the anguish of a woman living over something long past. Then low moaning less like pain than remorse for some unforgettable sin.

Seeing my light the night sister looks in. 'No,' in answer to my question, 'she's not really in pain – not physically, at least. As far as we can judge she's feeling nothing whatever.'

For all they know she cries for restful death.

'Put your book away, now.' She is a new sister. 'You should be sound asleep.' Yes?

I switch off my reading lamp.

'Four corners to my bed,
Four angels round my head.'

Too many things diminish me in this place. There are no angels round my bed these days.

Sunday☞ Sister Ariel is here. Pain . . . No opera, no ballet for me today. Not much breath either. A knotted cord tightens across my chest. Tighter. Sister has a fine touch with the pillows.

Wednesday☞ The last time Rose was here she

looked intently at me and then round the room and asked me how things were. It wasn't the moment for shattering details. I simply said, 'I could write a book about it.'

'Then why on earth don't you, my dear?' said Rose. 'I really mean it.'

Dear Rose. How to write inside these four walls? No communication to speak of.

Thursday Seven o'clock in the morning. Light creeps in stealthily. The window is wide open but the space is dark grey, as if it were a pane muffled in cobwebs. Five hundred meals in a row taken alone. There's nothing benign about this kind of solitude. It begins to be almost tangible with dimensions of its own. There must be hundreds of men and women all over the country who have to learn to live with it, when the mind wears so much better than the body. In this situation you never make a new acquaintance. Passing years spirit away some of the old ones. Distance, and bleak rooms like this one don't make it easy for people to come to you. And you can never go to them.

You can escape, and live by proxy in a book for five or six hours a day. But not all day and not every day. Or listen to the radio. Television? Yes, if you can take murder and mayhem, unlimited, and can enjoy the unconscious humour of daily hospital series.

Except for David, Helen's growing family seldom come here now. They are gay and enterprising. A day needs to be elastic to hold all they plan, and very often carry out. You don't need to be psychic to see that this environment subdues them.

But today, perceptive eight year old Vanessa came to see me. In some ways the child is shy, but she can be warm and outgoing, like Helen who brought her here. She began to dance for me, delightfully, but in clogs, which she explained were the 'in' thing at the moment. She then asked would I like to hear 'Alouette' and 'Click Go the Shears'? I would, indeed.

Helen and I looked at each other. We could see Vanessa was at work to break an evil spell. She didn't quite know what this was. But she was sensitive enough to try and do something about it. Lovely Vanessa. She'll never know the music her clattering clogs made for me on this repulsive linoleum.

Friday No comment.

Saturday Too many of these days are nightmares of infinite despair.

Monday September is nearly over. Not much spring about it. Just a rusty chain of days. Wind, more wind, and rain.

Tonight the curtain blows in, making grotesque shadows of familiar things. In the dim light they are a macabre frieze that dances along the wall opposite my bed, to the loud drumming of the rain.

The new sub-matron makes no pretence of trying to replace Sister MacHeath. She has an appalling memory. She is charming and pretty. Only eight months married, and more wife than matron.

Tuesday My favourite night nurse looks like Hattie Jacques who sometimes makes the absurd so entertaining. Nurse has the same clear, smooth voice, too. It is very persuasive. For her, as for me, 'a garden is a lovesome spot'. Last week she was amazed to hear I'd never seen tasselled parsley, and tonight she brings me a handsome bouquet of it from her own garden.

Wednesday Still 'too cold' outside. Bed is, indeed, the Word here. For many it may be the only possibility. But a G.P. should be able to convince any matron that even a terminal patient can enjoy fresh air with a little shelter. My behaviour patterns are all wrong for a hag-ridden world.

Thursday First light and foggy. But by mid-morning sun glitters on the iron roof outside my window. Sister Tyrone rugs me up and wheels me on to the two-by-four verandah outside. Lively snatches of dialogue waft over from the kitchen a yard or so away. Two voices are flat but highpitched. The other is Irish, but without the soft lilt.

The sun wouldn't melt an icecream. Still, it's good to look at. In less than half an hour it is gone. A small wind comes curling up the three wooden steps. And so to bed.

Friday Already light at half past six today. People with gardens will watch green shoots break through the earth up towards the sun – daffodils, hyacinths, narcissus – and primrose, 'lovely first born child of spring'.

This afternoon Doris brings me a most special bouquet from her own garden. Palest pink rhododendrons, with one rare cerise bloom in the centre, wrapped in a lacy frill of sweet-smelling white jasmine. They make you forget your constant view of that maze of wires and waterpipes that cuts across your strip of sky, which is no bigger than a pillow case.

Saturday Some mysterious skin infection plagues me fore and aft. Never before has my skin suffered even an adolescent pimple.

October

Monday These traumatic months have taught

me to swallow more than one ungilded philosophic pill. But whatever the odds against them, from office to kitchen, all the staff are kind.

Margaret, already a grandmother she tells me as, looking incredibly young, she mops the floor, and keeps my room as bright as it can be – if you take into account the motley odds and ends she has to work on. She's buoyant, secure, happy and friendly. Yet, closing down on me like dense fog over a bleak landscape, the unspeakable, ambivalent realities of this place begin to possess me.

Tuesday Pain. That knotted cord is tightening. More all-embracing pain. Weariness. My hold on life is slackening.

Wednesday Today, my G.P. This skin infection is obstinate and not at all easy to take. He looks grave and calls it a fungus. My previous acquaintance with fungi is strictly limited to mushrooms, to which I am extremely partial. But they are not to be had in this part of the woods.

Turning to Sister Spencer and looking deep in thought, he says, 'I think Miss Newton needs a holiday, Sister.'

Her smile tells me she couldn't agree with him more. Possibly she thinks as I do, that I've picked up the infection in the primitive, noisome place they call the shower room. So sometimes evil can be good. At once my G.P. says he will get me a room at Prince Edward's. They will give me intensive care for a while.

Thursday Sister tells me they are going to move someone very old into this room when I leave. She is stone deaf. And she is blind. They will be good to her. And nature has seen to it that her senses will not be flayed by sights and sounds that have played the devil with me.

Friday ☞ Tomorrow morning I go back to Prince Edward's. The trauma of the last six months is indelible. So are the skill and the expert care and compassion in the midst of what might be called every natural disadvantage and despair. I'll remember Sister MacHeath and Sister Tyrone. And Sister May, slim as willow, smiling all through night duty, with five girls and boys asleep at home, dealing with pain, swift as a flying-fish darting from sea to upper-deck, with that injection. And the outgoing young nursing-aide who delights in giving me a touch of glamour. Off-duty, today she brings her handsome small son and daughter to meet me.

Now solid brick walls will deaden piteous sounds. For me there will be the sun, moon and stars. And below a street where the world is always passing by – and trees.

Above all, at Prince Edward's there is gentle rest.

PRINCE EDWARD'S

Friday⟋ Late violets and early boronia from Kate and Sybil waiting for me on my table. And a most ingenious folding book-rest, too. Light and easy to handle. Sprays of dark green leaves and paler green elm-flowers border the whole fabric that covers it, with a wandering sage-green ribbon to bind them into a garland. In the centre four finely traced lilac broken stripes and through them a scatter of starry dark leaves and elm-blossom. Kate made it for me. Sheer inspiration.

Saturday⟋ Close to my hand one quiet purr from the telephone. I lift the receiver. It's Helen – who else? – to wish me good morning. In the afternoon she comes to see me with the first strawberries.

Sunday⟋ No visitors. But in the distance there's sounding brass and singing bringing colour to the Gardens. Towards evening my cardiologist, Ian McTavish – kilt swirling, bonnet a-tilt, streamlined case in one hand and under his free arm – bagpipes. McTavish is *not* his name, and all the rest is pure fantasy, except the essential case. But without bonnet or kilt he has panache. He must know everything about him is handsome. Yet, if he suspects the rapture his visits call forth from some of the younger nurses, he doesn't admit it by as much as a flick of an eyelid. He often walks up several flights of the stone steps of the fire escape and through the balcony door. To prove he still can? Perhaps. Because it's Sunday he's in comfortable brown tweeds and yellow jumper. Helen says he has only to put his head inside my door and I'm well. So I am, for an exquisite hour – and even think a drive along the Great Ocean Road is a possibility, or a few days in the Grampians that already must be a vast tapestry of wildflowers.

Without ringing for Sister my doctor deftly unpacks, and finds the nearest power-point for his machine. Then quickly and very gently fixes the various leads in places where they will have most to tell him in his E.C.G. A warm word about Dylan Thomas – he'll never let me 'go gently into the good night'. That is all. The room is empty.

Monday ⫽ Breakfast. Grapefruit. Poached egg. Marmalade or honey. Toast. And my own firm little pat of butter to spread on it. Coffee – all served in the style to which I'd nearly hardened myself to being unaccustomed.

A knock on my door at 8.15. 'Want an *Age*, love?' It is Herbert, Prince Edward's paper-boy for the last twenty years. On my five or six previous appearances here, he has supplied me with daily papers. Also his personal, well-seasoned items of social comment. With hundreds, maybe thousands passing through here every year, it amazes me that he always re-members my particular choice of daily.

'Yer nearly didn't get yer paper, today.' There's drama here.

'How is that?'

'Been knocked down by a "hit and run".'

'Herbert!' I hope I rose to the occasion. 'He should get "life" for doing a thing like that.'

'And he *would*,' says Herbert, 'Only 'e got away too fast for me to get 'is bloody number.'

My friend Herbert is a craggy veteran of World War II. He tells me he's going to retire, 'as soon as the

Repat. does the decent thing by him'. Nurse has drawn back the curtains to let in the morning sun. It's still a little tentative. But the heating is geared to a warm spring day.

Tuesday Sister Mead is back on duty. Unbelievably, she has me in my favourite fourth floor room again. It is only a very short time since she came with her camellias one bleak day to Haddon. Yet she gives me the impression that my sudden return here was more or less what she expected.

Reunion last night with Nurse Vlast. A treasure – more to me than gold. It is not so long since our last meeting. Yet she seems as happy to find me in my old bed as I am to be in it.

The fungus begins to fade. Sister Mead and Nurse Vlast make no comment. Their faces tell me what they might like to say. It is treated four-hourly round the clock. Already I no longer feel as if parts of me are lying on an ant-bed. I've no idea what balm they use, but no queen was ever more blissfully anointed.

Visitors and still more visitors. It must be a wonderful year for gardens. The shelf that runs almost the full length of one wall is like a hedge of roses – deep red, apricot, gold, pink and white with elegant, long-stemmed carnations, too. Much good sleep. And hours of waking that are calm and almost as restful as sleep itself.

Wednesday After six parched months the scent of new-mown grass blown towards me from the long nature-strip goes to my head as wine and strong waters have never done. Even the rasping whirr of the motor mower cannot destroy me. Far from grating on my ears, today, it is a magnificat.

Friday Out on the balcony. If the sun is still with us Sister invites me to take my lunch here. And winter changes in one day to spring. Above the balcony railing, over the way, seven elm trees promise big bouquets of summery green leaves, and birches have unfurled their velvet buds. The little two-storey terrace of Victorian villas has been discreetly renewed. A touch here and there to the facade, points to its old-time elegance. And they tell me it is now used as professional rooms in the more orthodox sense. No more dalliance.

Because of my sudden exit from Haddon, I am without books. There were far too many other items in this collector's harvest for Helen – how she must hate all this pack-and-follow business – to cope with. Some of my old friends on the staff have ransacked their own bookshelves for me. Their treasure is stacked beside me – *The Story of Civilisation,* exquisitely illustrated, *The Chateaux of the Loire, European Art and Architecture in the Eighteenth Century,* all a delight to handle and to be frequently tasted, perhaps more than read. Besides these, there's a fascinating *Life of Sir Malcolm Sargent.* Once, in my youth, I sat next to him at the theatre. I can see him now, shorter than one expected, but perfectly presented, down to the perennial red carnation in his buttonhole. To me he seemed very much alone. Quite possibly of his own choosing. He had no programme. I yearned to offer him mine. But I was too bashfully aware of this great occasion. Besides, my mother sat on my other side. And she was a pillar of the Never Talk to Strangers school.

There is a book about gardens and how you make them, too. The kind of gardening book you hope for, but have long given away expectation of finding.

November

Monday☞ How quickly the weeks have slipped into November. Suddenly I'm aware that for a month I've not heard one pitiful, mindless cry. There are a few very old patients here, but not one illness is debited to the crime of being old. Here they take old age for what it is – a stage in transit. But not a disease. A fact of life.

Half my allotted time here has almost melted away. There are other men and women with terminal illness, too. Like me they can stay no longer than three months. They need expert care from time to time, but they can enjoy a game of chess, sometimes amble along a sunlit balcony or garden path, and pass the time of day with their peers. Or even carve a little wooden boat to delight some child. Environment is not everything. But this place is buoyant. It's a little world where, even if you will soon 'fear no more the heat o' the sun, Nor the furious winter's rages,' you are still a human being. You still have your own life beyond the limits of any casebook. Something seems to say you may not be immortal. But Life is. There's a feeling of continuity, and you are part of it. Soon Helen will be here. I must finish copying out the recipe of that ambrosial potato salad I promised her from Sister's fabulous book about a garden.

Tuesday☞ Bird's song brings in the day. A flush of flamingo cloud as the sun rises. All round my room there are flowers.

Wednesday☞ Mrs McMintie, our one-time daily help, to see me. She brings me some exquisite pink carnations. She has often brought me a few flowers which she arranges beautifully, taking plenty of time. She much prefers a flower in hand to duster or mop. Why not? She's loyal – an earth-mother type who scarcely makes a move, except in the way of kindness.

Friday☞ That old hag Angina is catching up with me again. Sister pours brandy into a tubby little glass Niels brought me from Sweden. Puts it in my hand and patters away for the injection.

'Fifteen men on a dead man's chest,
Yo-ho-ho and a bottle of rum.'

This was no dead man's chest. It was mine, with the weight of the world on it. Tight. And breathless. Pain... The windows.

'Please. Wide open.'

Sister with morphine. Then the prick. It doesn't bring oblivion as it did once. Just a don't care feeling. And a vague awareness that the battle must be fought again... How calm and good they are to me... So quiet... And a fresh wind blowing.

Monday☞ November nearly over. Kate and Sybil to see me again. Almost every week they've come for nearly five years now. Much to talk of – for we are to books as locusts are to the choicest crops.

We agree that our devotion to Trollope and his Palliser and Barchester novels lasts because every time we pick up one of his books we're in close touch with men and women. Kate and Sybil supply me with most of the reading I need. And delightful it is. It's a fine thing to have young siblings who send their wishes for Christmas and birthdays with most tactfully chosen books.

Friday☞ My T.V. tells me Christmas is in the air. A more and more competitive Christmas. There seems to be a larger than life Santa handing out hidden persuasion to the young in every big store in city and suburb.

Sunday A surprise visit from an eighty-three-year-old acquaintance today. A superb gardener. By a wave of the hand, her only daughter says, she has turned hundreds of dollars into exquisite rhododendrons, azaleas, camellias, carnations and roses. She waters, sprays and prunes them all at need. She tends her own compost heap. 'Always put back into the soil what you take out of it, dear.' Her garden grows by her own hand, completely unaided, except for the man who comes once a week to mow the lawns. And she knows every plant you can mention by its given name and species.

Today she has brought me a charming little bouquet she has arranged with a very special strain of pansies and just one late sprig of her lily of the valley in the centre. 'Autumnal grace', if ever I've known it.

Monday Cup-week has come and gone. My friend Herbert tells me of a few 'good things' he's whipped home at Flemington and says nothing of the bad ones. This morning a rare shave and hair-cut, and bright yellow shirt with blue and gold tie, like someone's racing colours, suggest that he has prospered.

December

Wednesday Christmas. The holly and the ivy. Nurses, off-duty, deck wards and corridors with toy Christmas trees, leaves, baubles, lanterns and tinsel garlands. My room is a garden of lilies. Some wrapping and much more unwrapping of gifts. No visitors. All are much too busy. Except the one and only Helen. The narrow door of my wardrobe has become a stained glass window. Taped to it are really beautiful cards.

Three or four groups of unaccompanied carol singers come at the end of the day and stroll from floor to floor with 'The First Noel', 'Away in a Manger', hearty 'Good King Wenceslas' and 'God Rest You Merry, Gentlemen'. The bird-like voices of children in one choir are very touching.

Friday And so to Christmas Eve. Dusk, gently enjoyable without lights. A rustling at my door. Subdued laughter. Then a knock. My niece Veronica, my nephew Adam and the three pretty daughters of a prettier mother – Emma first, fifteen, Virginia a year or so younger. And my friend Vanessa – eight years plus. Festively attired? Oh no. Faded blue jeans and T-shirts all. Vanessa's is white, printed with a very red Jonathan and the legend 'I love Apples', Virginia in her favourite blues and violets, Emma more restrained and slightly more tailored, as usual. Veronica, easy to look at as ever, in a sophisticated shirt-blouse. Adam, too, is decorative in tangerine and black. They bring me a sack of gifts. From Veronica and Adam a fascinating book about the making of Victorian cities. Emma and the two V's have designed and made their separate gifts in the craft room. A padded box for my 'jewels' (Virginia). A gem of a housewife in an abstract black and white design, complete with needles, thread, tape-measure and scissors (Emma) and from Vanessa a parcel elaborately tied with scarlet velvet ribbon, and in it a heart-shaped pincushion to match, a ribbon embossed with white butterflies for it to hang on, and enough fine pins with confetti coloured heads to fill my needs for several years.

'We know you love music, Auntie,' says Virginia, the impresario, 'so we've brought you a concert.' After this how dare Helen suggest that my geese are not really swans?

Recorders are produced by Emma and Vanessa, and carols take over. 'On the First Day of Christmas', 'Good King Wenceslas', 'Noel, Noel', 'The Holly and the Ivy'. Like wood-pigeons, the lovely notes of every descant flew all around me. And then my special favourite, 'Greensleeves'. Of all things possible, nothing in the world could have given me the same joy, their thought, the secret planning, and the performance.

'The piano is too big to bring in here. Instead, we've brought the cassette and some tapes,' says Virginia, proudly, 'so that you can hear Vanessa play.' And play she does. A lovely Bach *Minuet*, and a gay colourful *Country Dance* of Bartok's. Music flows through Vanessa's veins from her head and heart to her shapely, strong, small hands. We could hear her own joy in her playing, even though it was taped. Much applause, a little very light refreshment, and our revels ended. Never once since the day my G.P. sentenced me, in this very room, had I even imagined that my heart could ever beat again in time to such happiness.

The simplicity and the unspoken tenderness of it said all I needed to know this strange Christmas day.

Saturday Christmas this year is a kind of aura. Neither an hour nor a day. A pretty lavender-bag and well-wishing card from the hospital on my breakfast tray. Midday comes awareness that for a whole week a heroic chef has been adventuring among turkeys, hams and plum-pudding. And he doesn't forget a scatter of almonds and raisins and crystallized fruits as well.

Not a visitor today. I'm as alone as a mirror. Helen cannot leave her country family who are covering three hundred miles in the day to be with her for Christmas-tree and dinner with all the rest.

January

Monday✎ Already into the New Year. The bright days left to me at Prince Edward's can be counted on my two hands.

Helen has given me a filmy white housecoat, powdered with red, blue, white and yellow field flowers. I tell her I'm past this delightful frippery which is fit for a trousseau.

Tuesday✎ Sister Mead says, airily, but with a hint of persuasion, 'Have you made a will?'

'No, Sister. Have you?'

'Of course I have,' she says. 'Everyone should.'

'Helen is my only next of kin. My vast estate will go to her. Or her children. There's no need for me to make a will, Sister.'

'It might save your sister a lot of trouble later on, you know. Besides, you've got a few very nice bits and pieces. You might like to leave them to special people. You think about it. Let me know in a day or two if you want me to ring your solicitor.'

'I'll think about it,' I said. Meaning I've already done my thinking.

'No worries, my dear. Lawyers never mind coming to the hospital you know,' says Sister.

I think. About Sister Mead. This suggestion of hers is completely out of character. Besides, there have been two or three other times when making my will would have been much more to the point than it is today. Though innocent of trick or plot, Sister has been prompted by somebody. Helen? *Never*. Who then?

With a fixed income of about half nothing – minus inflation – to make a will seems to me slightly ostentatious.

Wednesday Enter Sister to see if I've finished thinking over her suggestion. I'm tempted to ask her if it's really hers? Instead, I give her my solicitor's phone number and ask her to invite him to come and see me. She looks pleased that her part is finished. 'It will make things easy for you if you jot down anyone or anything you particularly want to remember, before he comes.'

I intend Helen to have all I own that is worth having. Yet there are still a few old treasures left for the children and two or three old friends. If only there were more to give them. Meanwhile I toil and trouble. Another page into the waste paper basket. Another. And still another. And all this need never have happened. Not that making a will brings death nearer. At any odds it's just as natural as birth. And a puff of wind doesn't make all that much difference to a candle burning at both ends.

Strangely, the thought of extinction doesn't harrow me today as it once did. But I must tell someone this lady's not for burning. I'd much rather lie out and far in a still, green paddock near the Dividing Range. As the seasons pass, there can be worse things than becoming part of that loveliness. Worse things than changing into grass where sheep can safely graze. And I rather like the thought of my dust coming back to earth from eternity in a tall, shade-giving tree.

This week has been very humid and oppressive. After a good shower or two it is cooler now, and the trees are lifting up their heads, dewy with rain. Still thinking I watch the sun set. Strange little flamingo clouds flock in the heavy, dark grey background of sky beside and beyond the cathedral. At dusk, from my lookout here there's always something good to see. Through black sky an interstate plane flashes down towards Tullamarine.

Friday This morning a nice young man comes from the solicitor to draft my will. He's the legal head of the skeleton staff left to make the old firm available to its clients in the long vacation.

Sunday Helen with flowers and fruit. Not many visitors this week. Most people seem to be out of town. Though Kate and Sybil are constant as ever.

February

Monday This seems to be the month for tightening loose knots. This morning, Matron, who, in the midst of the hospital's problems, still manages to help with mine, too, sends a social worker to see me, to discuss my 'housing' problem. She's an experience. Very good-humoured, spare, but wiry, she seems wound up by a spring of tremendous vitality. It's hard to believe she has three children, one an academic, and two others well on the way. She's dashing and cheerful, functional, too. I listen, slightly breathless, half expecting her next remark to be 'Who's for hockey, girls?'. She's already in touch with my G.P. Now that my time at Prince Edward's has run out, they have booked a room for me for Thursday at Cumberland House. It is a small but very well-known hospital on the other side of the river. 'Much nearer your sister, you know. And no parking problems.' They will keep me at Cumberland House for a maximum of six weeks. Within that time, a room is promised me in yet another of these nursing homes where old ladies go to die. Geographically, at least, this will not be so far from home as Haddon.

Tuesday This afternoon the nice young man brings the will he drafted ready for me to sign. Slowly and very patiently he reads it to me to make sure it truly embodies my wishes. The care, elaboration and elegance of phrasing seem to give me millionaire status, at least, for the time being.

Then two copies are duly signed before witnesses. One he has for safe keeping. The other is with me. Now no more devising and bequeathing. But no sooner is he gone than I'm convinced that not half the bequests are at all as I would like them to be. I should have stood by my first intention and departed with no will, and no regrets.

April

Thursday My last day here. Those nightmare months at Haddon have thrust too deeply into my mind and senses to be forgotten. But after this golden summer, their scars no longer smart.

Time, that for all those months I tried to kill, is no longer my enemy. Now, there is good in every hour. With all their skills and compassion, this is Prince Edward's gift.

This morning there's another round of my annual 'final farewells'. The nurses who have cared so well for me make up the tally of my previous departures. And laughing they refuse to say 'good-bye'.

'Oh, you'll be back with us again,' is their last word. They seem to feel an impulse to talk. As they would to put heart into any old friend doomed to sail, again and again, into unknown seas.

CUMBERLAND HOUSE

Thursday Cumberland House is solid red brick and a thought or two less romantic than its name. But full of light and fresh air. My room is in the new wing. No view, but the window brings in the sun for a good part of the day. This gives a soft glow to white walls that seem to be newly painted.

The furniture is light-coloured natural wood, polished and contemporary without being stark. There's a dressing-table, comfortable bed, built-in wardrobe, a small writing-table and a very welcoming chair. Nothing to suggest a room in a hospital, except the odds and ends on the inevitable bedside locker. The dressing-table is very roomy, though not too big for the room. An oblong mirror runs across its full width. This makes a reflecting pool for the masses of flowers that fill the table. It's like a miniature indoor garden today.

Friday On a small scale Cumberland House is exceedingly well planned and presented. This includes the staff, all young and friendly. Too young in their profession for their aureoles of dedication to be a scrap tarnished by wear and tear.

Tuesday There's always a feeling here that life goes on. Leading surgeons keep the theatres busy. There's no flurry. A kind of steady round, like an escalator. Plenty of to-and-fro, yet everything seems perfectly timed. You begin to feel almost like a minor 'extra', in a small, but superbly directed documentary film. Sometimes I half expect a loud voice to say

'Take'.

Sunday Helen to see me, as ever. At least it's easier to come here than battle through city peak-hour traffic. She and Virginia have, as of old, shared the usual, joint dinner-party celebration of their birthdays, which are only two days apart. Last night Virginia had her boy and girl party for the young. Veronica and Adam, who are the kind of parents one sometimes reads about, retired to a den upstairs. The revellers took possession below.

Tuesday Sybil and Kate bring me books and two gardenias from their own little tree that shelters by their front porch. Friendship can go no further than parting with those cosseted gardenias, as I well know.

Friday This has been a good week of visits, letters and flowers. There's something special about autumn roses – because we know they are about to vanish for the winter. Sister Mead to see me – with a 'bouquet of black olives'.

Sunday Perhaps because of all the flowers round me, Virginia keeps coming to my mind. She has escaped early adolescent lumpiness. Helen says she looks prettier than ever, with that elusive grace all her own. She reminds me of the girls in Shakespeare's comedies – especially Perdita.

Tuesday I miss my lovely view from Prince Edward's. But it's never dull here. There's a feeling of plenty of action, yet it's divinely restful. Even though there is an old character next-door who calls very frequently for her sister or daughter. As I thought. It is her *dog* she really calls, so they tell me.

Wednesday Nothing here suggests even remotely the lovely surroundings I've enjoyed all this summer. But pain has not been too often with me. And when it has been, skill, and awareness of my need have quickly taken over.

Thursday Once more Helen packs for me. This afternoon the caravan moves off on yet another stage of these odd, inevitable little journeys.

The measure of my happiness at Cumberland House is, that though very different in tradition and scale from Prince Edward's, in so many ways it holds to just the same good uses of the world. The three and a half weeks have almost danced away.

DAWSON TOWERS

May

Friday Veronica insists on driving Helen and me in her roomy new station waggon. My new destination bears a name that suggests nothing if not stately homes and landed gentry. Its facade is triple-fronted, solid, pink brick, with sundry red-tiled gables and numerous gargoyles to match.

I have a good view because we have to wait to make room for two or three cars that are leaving, to pass. From the front, it is late-Edwardian-Queen Anne, set in a small, unkempt patch of lawn with a struggling tree or two. It may have made its mark in Robin Boyd's *Great Australian Ugliness*. On one side is a massive concrete carpark. We go inside, past a small lounge, its end wall almost filled by the biggest television set I've ever seen, and a couple of windows that do not exactly sparkle in the afternoon light. Along each of the other two walls, there is a row of vacant, unsmiling faces facing each other. Their owners sit in big chairs, wedged leg to leg, with not an inch to spare, as if they have all been drilled into keeping those two straight, inflexible lines for ever and ever.

There are no doors to the lounge. It is open on to a wide corridor with several private rooms on either side. Walls and vinyl-covered floor are that uniform, greyish, flat colour that has fixed itself indelibly in my mind as nursing-home white. This wing is an addition. It has a prefabricated, do-it-yourself air. Inside my room, which is at the end of the corridor, Helen turns to me and says, 'Darling, do you really think the name...?' We laugh.

Saturday My room. The walls are clean and it's well enough lit if you burn its two small lights for most of the day. In shape it is not unlike a single cabin on one of the old coasters that used once to sail so pleasantly round to Sydney. Forget that it has a window, instead of a porthole looking out on to the sea, and no curtains. There is a tatty blind instead.

From the window there's not a glimpse of sky. Cars are parked foursquare across it. Except one corner where you can see a few feet of bare, solid tree-trunk. It could be any very old tree. There's not a branch or a leaf in sight to say what it is. There is also a noisome incinerator. It is hidden from sight on two sides by a tea-tree fence and is wide open to the view from my bed.

My room has about as much humanity in it as a parallelogram – no mirror, no shelf or table of any kind to hold a book or a single flower. Not even a hook or a rail where one could hang a print. But there is a small cupboard for hanging clothes. Beside the bed there is just enough space to open the door into the shower room and toilet. They call this a duplex and it is shared with the patient next door. In it there is a cupboard, the door of which is a mirror. It is placed so high on the wall that if you are of average height you have no hope of seeing anything below your eyebrows reflected in it. The towel rail is broken at one end.

The hot water service is a fiery spring. Happily, for a quick glance at basin and shower recess tells me both will need a good scalding to make them usable. Nurse says to ring my bell if there is anything I need. The bell has been out of order since my arrival. So has the power point for a T.V. set.

Helen comes with purple grapes, oranges, figs and black olives, as well as this morning's *Age*. She sits by me in a curious chair, with a skeleton back, a padded seat and straight wooden arms about four inches wide. It looks as though its maker intended to upholster it and then suddenly changed his mind.

Helen says she will bring my bookshelves and some books as well. There will be a place for a small bowl of flowers then. Possibly a print, too. It may be the complete absence of the faintest hint of colour that lets a rank mist of stark isolation lie over this room.

June

Sunday Today is one of Helen's good days, when she is involved with family. I don't want them to come here. This is not their world. Too chilling a heritage for them to know of – even by inference. Although it's Sunday, there does not seem to be much visiting. When you are outside the mainstream of living, ties are broken. This sense of solitude is one of the things that the *haves* do not escape. Nor do the *have-nots* in these little nursing homes, which as Daisy Ashford said of Edward VII's crown, are 'small but costly'. In one way all handicapped people are alike. They will never live again as average men and women do. That is what bring us to havens of doubt and shadowy despair like this same Dawson Towers. Already there's an end-of-the-road feeling all round me in this small room. At least when the bell tolls there's nothing under this roof that will make it hard to leave. Pretty thought for a grey day ...

Monday Early this morning Matron, who has been on week-end leave, comes to see me. I mention my persistently silent bell. She seems disturbed that she has not heard of this before and says she will have it fixed today. Already we seem on the same wavelength. Even on this short acquaintance she makes me think there are sundry things she would like to change in this narrow world that looks to her for help. Between pauses, an impression filters through that there is very little she can do because of a tangential, outside force – the proprietor. Like many registered nursing homes, Dawson Towers is run as an investment.

Matron is impressive. A tall big-boned woman, with well drawn features and fine dark eyes. Put in her knot of silky, black hair a high Spanish comb and over it a black lace mantilla, and she is Dona Ana to an eyelash. She seems warm and outgoing, with plenty of spirit, and a sense of humour. This, after only a couple of days here, I suspect she often needs.

An hour later a lean man with a small kit-bag arrives. He looks shabby. I wish him 'good morning'. He makes some sound. Perhaps it's 'good morning', but it's unlike any language I've ever heard before. He opens his kit-bag, takes out a screwdriver, some screws, and a length of cord, and sets to work on my bell. After considerable patience, and much testing, it eventually rings. He then tinkers with the power-point for a few minutes. This he does not test. I thank him and without a word, still hatted, he departs.

Nurse brings my lunch on a brown tray with four short legs, just like a dachshund. 'Your bell is fixed,' she says. 'I saw the proprietor come in here. He does all the odd jobs round the hospital.'

Lunch. It would be adequate, but only just, for a three-year old. There is, in addition to the main course, a milk pudding with cream, and a glass of milk. No alternative is offered. But Helen's grapes and figs from the very small Chinese basket, that with lamp, waterjug and glass just manages to fit on my bedside locker, keep me from being really hungry.

Tuesday My second brand-new cake of elegant French bath soap that was an unexpected birthday gift has vanished from the shower room. This morning I collect soap, talc, washers, toothbrush and paste in my sponge-bag. There is nowhere else to put them, so I hang the bag from the drawer-knob of the bedside locker. On Sister's advice, my belongings will no longer be left in the shower room.

Day begins here at 5 a.m. No early morning cup of tea. Breakfast at 7.30. The main meal is at midday. There is afternoon-tea poured into your cup as your nursing-aide of the moment likes it, and handed to you from a trolley in the hall. There seem to be only three full-time members of staff – Matron, the charge sister, and a nursing-aide. Her name is Sarah. She's a tall, slender, very beautiful girl who comes from one of the Pacific Islands. Nurse Sarah is charmingly spoken, and said to be a fully qualified sister in her own country, but this training is not recognized here. The other members of staff are recruited from agencies and come and go – mostly go – for one or two sessions a week. Some I would say are not of Matron's choosing.

Wednesday More than an hour since Helen went. It seems like a day. Soon those cries, that wound more senses than just your hearing, will begin. For some unfathomable reason my door cannot be tightly closed against them.

I wish for alluring Madame Renoir, sitting in the garden, in her scarlet hat with the turned up brim, and demure black frock, which has no ornament but a knot of flowers. She looks as if she knows they lead the eye to her shapely bosom, and so to a glimpse of her very trim waist. Beside her is her enchanting small daughter in white frock and big flowery hat. This lets you see blue eyes, set wide apart, looking in delightful wonder at the world before her. There seems to be a summer garden of trees in the background. And between them they hold a flat basket that gives an impression of flowers and fruit. I imagine Madame looking straight into this room. Do I see a slight shudder? Perhaps not. But I'm sure those expressive silk-covered shoulders would give just a tiny shrug.

Things imagined and created, like Madame and the child, the flowers, rows of books and shelves can only underline the stark ugliness of this cell. They must stand out as lonely as a mirror on the wall of an empty house. A house that has never been lived in, or ever known the least human touch.

Thursday Television in the lounge sounds non-stop at undreamt-of decibels from nine o'clock in the morning till final bedding-down time comes at half-past seven in the evening. Besides this, T.V.s are often tuned, in private rooms along the corridor, to three different stations. Even an iron door could not shut out this hideous uproar. These poor fellow-travellers must be all but stone-deaf. Yet noise, like a football match and races, seems to be relished for its own sake. It should be possible to turn on my own T.V. softly, at night. Helen has had it tested and the verdict is that it is performing perfectly, on all stations. It must be this power-point that is at fault. As this is something entirely in the hands of God and the proprietor, I've a feeling nothing will be done about it. Besides, judging by the dimness of the lights, as well, it may be that re-wiring needs to be done right through this wing.

Sunday ♫ Sybil and Kate to see me. Bliss. They bring me some enticing Victoriana: *Dearest Mama.*

Monday ♫ Matron comes to see me at least once a day. She also gives out the evening batch of sedatives even when, in theory, she is off duty.

The staff are mostly kind and considerate. Except last night. The storm-trooper of a sister on duty tramped ceaselessly up and down the uncarpeted corridor in heavy, outdoor boots every time bells and loud, mindless cries called for her attention. She and her equally raucous nursing-aide, kept shouting to each other all through the night, from one end of the hospital to the other. Probably on the principle that if all their patients were not stone-deaf, they should be. Both could easily be heard in Matron's quarters which are not in the main part of the building. I think they will not come again.

By 2 a.m. sleep was not for me. Much too weary to read. And there was nothing else to hurry on these wakeful, creeping hours to daylight.

Wednesday ♫ Staff recruited from agencies, on a day-to-day basis, come and go in a way that's slightly bewildering. After two weeks here, nearly all are complete strangers. Today, we're a small scale United Nations. Nurse Sarah from the Islands, even in this bleak spot, keeps the warmth and gentle dignity of her people. This is not given to most other nurses. One sister has Polish parents, but is naturalized and has scarcely a trace of accent. Another is Australian, married to a Lithuanian. The pleasant, smiling girl who brought my breakfast this morning, is Italian. I wish I could speak their language as they speak mine. Most of them are married with two or three children.

They come back to nursing for a couple of sessions a week. They are only working they tell me, to help with the children's schooling, and to make it possible for them, and sometimes even a husband, to go to a university later. They may never even have heard of Disraeli, but they stand with him for light, liberty and learning. These newcomers seem hungrier than we are for education. They make a lively, though fleeting cross-section. But probably not one, except the Italian girl, perhaps, will ever come inside my door again.

The odd transience of life at Dawson Towers makes me feel more than ever rootless. It's like perpetually changing trains. As if you are forever waiting at some remote, run-down railway siding for a train to take you back on to the main line. That train never comes. Yet if not Dawson Towers, then where?

Kate and Sybil to see me. Marvellous of them. With homegrown lemons, too.

Saturday A Jugoslav sister gives me the injection this morning to stir up my red corpuscles. She plies her needle well, but not with quite the same expertise as Matron. Her car, a later model, and more impressive at all points than Helen's, stands four-square across my window. She has an enviable hold on English. But there's no time for talk here.

Sunday It begins to look dusky and Helen leaves early to write her weekly letter. This she usually does at the last minute, and rushes every Sunday to post it to her country child, come flood, fire or pestilence. Persuasively, I say a word or two about fast driving.

'Don't extend yourself too much, darling. It's the "intent" that matters. If your letter is short, she'll be longing all the more for the next one.'

Helen laughs. For ten years and more, strikes permitting, her letter has never once missed Sunday's mail.

Monday�✍ A public holiday. In the lounge, television blasts the air with one sporting session after another. There's never a concord of sweet sound here. Three sets in rooms nearby are playing rock, race and football – *fortissimo*. Occasionally, a nurse, in desperation, lowers the volume in the lounge. Within minutes it is raised again to the very limit of decibels.

To call this head-splitting bedlam shattering is paltry understatement. It would make the perfect background in an *avant-garde* play for a scene set in hell. If only this drama and the meaningless cries of one of my near neighbours ended with the day. Ten hours is a long session. I wish, just for once, I could hear the soft sounds of nightfall: birds, and gentle rain, and rustling leaves.

Thursday�✍ Every morning on the stroke of nine, when no one is about, a compact little man with a neat Van Dyke beard, opens the entrance door, waste paper basket in hand. Then across my concrete landscape he cuts a perfect diagonal line to the incinerator two or three feet past my window. Deftly, with what looks like scientific precision, he empties whatever that basket holds, into the incinerator. He then goes back exactly as he has come. As if that diagonal line were chalked for him to follow over the concrete that is in ever-present need of sweeping and hosing. His build vaguely suggests a garden gnome in tweeds. He's no geriatric. There is almost a spring in his walk. He is not young, but he looks animated and alert and human. Something in his face makes you remember man's – and woman's – incomparable mind. But what does he bring with such care, day after day, in his waste paper basket, to commit to the flames? The rough draft of yesterday's chapter of his autobiography? It could be the tale of the dangers he had passed when he was on a geological search for oil, in New Guinea, Iran or Kuwait, perhaps. Or trial and error solutions of some problem that has possessed him for half a lifetime. One thing seems certain. His place is no more here than mine is.

Some debate with Helen on the importance of not visiting this cheerless place three times a week. Warmly she refuses my persuasion. She brings me the first daffodils, a couple of camellias, a sprig or two of daphne. They look just like spring.

Friday⁊ Nurse, with an eye on my clip-board and the scribble in tatty old diaries or on backs of envelopes that I'm trying to tailor into readable pages:

'What are you writing?'

'My diary,' I reply, completely off-guard. This is unfortunate. I have been questioned often enough before but usually find myself answering with the trite refrain: 'Just a letter to an old friend.'

Monday⁊ More than ever in a cage today, I put on something warm and amble up the corridor as far as the lounge. Their T.V. for once, is silent – a good time to make this first excursion outside my own door in many weeks. Books light my darkness. But desperate need to communicate with people in flesh and blood, alive, outside the printed page drives me on this not so joyous errand. It is partly to break through the isolation of one room, but hoping, too, for some slight acquaintance with the Knight of the Waste Paper Basket. Every chair is filled. He is not there. Not a soul answers my hopeful, 'Good-morning, how-are-you?' with the sketch of a smile, much less a word.

Sunflowers turn to the light. Not one of these human beings makes the least move to reach for the small enriching things that are still within their grasp.

Matron comes on her good-night round. I ask her about the man with the waste paper basket.

'Mr Defris? Oh, he's in a ward with one old gentleman who never leaves his bed.'

'He looks as if he might be interesting.'

'He's always pleasant,' says Matron. 'He has his own desk and lives entirely in his room. He seems quite contented.'

Perhaps. To me he suggests the classic instance of a man alone, who is able, intelligent and ambulant. Because of illness, he needs a certain amount of continuing expert care. So there is nowhere but a psycho-geriatric nursing home for him to go. And he wouldn't be given a bed that a thousand other men and women are waiting for if he did not need it. So Mr Defris and I are both marooned among the wreckage of Dawson Towers.

Tuesday This happens to be a very occasional heavy week of bridge for Helen. She will not be here till the day after tomorrow.

Rose is back from Paris and Dublin. Looking well and very *soignée*, she comes to see me this afternoon. She brings me dewy violets and a print, already framed, of Cézanne's. It is mostly exquisite greens, a bridge you can almost walk through to the other side, still waters, and a few waterlilies. This light is not kind to it, but even so, it does my soul good, as Helen's youngest daughter said to me when she tasted her first slice of water-melon.

Rose talks about music and theatre in Paris,

Dublin and London, and does it well. It's easy to understand why so many of this generation's gifted young can't get abroad quickly enough to try their wings. After she is gone something of her gift for living stays with me for a while.

But that gallery of faces in the lounge is still with me. Everyone wears the tragic mask of isolation that clings to unhappy old age. Much of it is tied up with situations that shouldn't be too difficult to change. A small, unregimented space – with no T.V. – to share a pot of tea and gossip with a friend who still calls you by your first name. There might be a quiet corner where you can play dominoes or draughts, do a jig-saw puzzle or smoke a pipe and talk about cricket and old times. There's no place for quiet talk, or even to write a letter here.

Some of these very people in the lounge may have small skills they could enjoy using. But in these places there's no design for living. Some old people have great wisdom, mellowed by time and long experience. Why not let them use it, meaningfully? Simply to exist is not living.

I lie back and remember Prince Edward's Sister Jo, intelligent, attractive in so many ways – all that a nurse can ever hope to be, with the purest Dublin English, as well. One day, when reading was not for me, Sister Jo brought her cassette over from the nurses' home and set it up with the complete tapes of Micheál Macliammóir in *The Importance of Being Oscar* – his fabulous, one-man Wilde extravaganza. We became friends in the beginning when I told her that her beautiful accent reminded me of him. Listening to Macliammóir's voice it seemed to me a good day, after all. But oh this never-ending June.

July

Thursday🌀 Two nursing-aides, slightly past their first youth, come regularly for one afternoon session a week. They arrive together in a banana-coloured car. With its bonnet pointed towards my room, it is always parked by some kind of pre-emptive right in precisely the same spot.

Invariably both come together to bring my afternoon tea, and return together, to collect my empty cup. Sometimes they bring my evening meal, also together. Today, my water-bottle is empty, and I ring for water to help me swallow a tablet. A quarter of an hour later both arrive with the concise query: 'What d'you want?' After a short time they bring me the necessary water. Yes – together again. I've never once heard either of their names. Strictly to each other Helen and I call them 'This' and 'That'. You don't need to be clairvoyant to see that they expect all patients to be senile. They prefer them that way. So do a few other nurses. 'This' and 'That' make no bones of letting me know I'm a cuckoo in this nest. They are a very odd pair. But for better or for worse, it must take a well-tuned mental and emotional make-up to be a good nurse in a place like Dawson. Hours are long. No one can find it easy to face the boredom of this kind of changeless routine day in, day out. There's never the challenge here that lends interest, even excitement, to exacting duty in ward or theatre at a modern hospital.

Friday🌀 Nearly every day the proprietor oozes in and out, like a genie from a bottle in one of those old Arabian fairy tales.

It must take all the selflessness, and sense of humour, as well as expertise, this fine forthcoming Matron has, to cope with these visitations. She could do better for herself than this. What draws me to her in this homeless dark is that she treats me as an individual. Not just as one more foiled, viewless wanderer in a maze that has been planned with a narrow way in, and no way out.

Saturday Helen with Amanda, who brings me a little jar of her special cumquat jam to grace my breakfast tray. It is made with fruit from her own garden.

Something in their visit makes me think about the importance of being in love, the love of home. Solitude is the one thing I'll never love. Today the cheerful, volatile social worker who put me here comes to see me. This month an Italian boy, a paraplegic, is coming to Dawson to give his parents the chance of their first real holiday in twenty years. 'He's a nice boy. Twenty-two and quite intelligent,' says the social worker. 'He has his own wheel-chair. Will you let him come along and talk to you?'

'Of course I will. But why send him here, among all these old people?'

'No one else will take him.'

'Surely he could go somewhere among patients nearer his own age.'

'Sadly no. It would be easier if he were a quadraplegic.'

'No room at the inn.' A pause, heavy with thought for both of us. Then, 'I wish I were nearer his own vintage. But let him come and see me. It will at least be someone for him to talk to.' 'Thank you, my dear,' she says. 'I thought you would help me help him.'

With a question or two about my own well-being,

to which my reply is mostly 'no comment', she goes on her way, good-hearted and buoyant as ever. I have a cold. Breathing problems. My doctor is to see me sometime today.

Later – By stealth, it seems, a most active virus has attacked my chest. Matron is here. She and my kind young G.P. fix me sitting bolt upright, stacking more and more pillows at my back. And so what seems a slightly lavish antibiotic routine begins.

Helen in bed with a cold, too. But, most happily, not the same brand as mine. 2 a.m. Another witches' sabbath begins. Next door but one those same incessant, non-human cries again. There must be some unreachable torment in a mind that is too pitifully maimed to cope with it. These are cries of mingled protest and menace. They have a ragged, bellowing sound. Nurse manages to quieten her a little. Those cries again. The voice is incredibly strong. Louder, louder and louder. The same raucous, petulant, cries. Please. *Please*, let this be enough. Let it stop. That sound fills my room. It pierces me through and through.

Beside me, on the locker, is a little bottle of tablets. It's always beside me. In red letters its label says, 'CAUTION. To be used strictly as directed by a physician.' I hold it in my hand. 'Two sublingually every four hours.' Yes, *two*. But eight – twelve – twenty – all at once ... ?

Helen – Veronica – David – the other children ... They would have to know I'd let thought dig my grave. Most deliberately I stretch my arm till that small bottle of mortality is pushed well out of easy reach.

Not many years ago I told someone that I would never 'go gentle into the dark night'. But where else is there to go? Where in all this world?

The dreadful cries have stopped. A strange silence. There is death in it.

Monday July is half over. Propped up on sundry pillows I held this pose by the wide open window for a couple of weeks.

By day, Matron herself took care of me, as no one else here could. The nights were a different story. At about half-past nine a nurse would bring me a cup of hot water, into which went one of Helen's soup cubes. This had been ordered for me last year to take with my five nightly tablets. This was all I ever saw of our night staff. Perhaps they looked at my chart, thought I might have Asian 'flu and wouldn't risk catching it.

One night I do remember. Weary with breathlessness and incessant coughing that nobody seemed to notice, and feeling very much alone, at last at 3 a.m. I rang my bell. The pretty, young night sister came and answered in reply to the request: '*Please*, could I have a cup of tea.' 'No dear, you couldn't possibly have a cup of tea at this hour. It's three o'clock.' She then very quickly departed. So my solo performance continued till morning, with every hour noted on my companionable little clock. I got my longed-for drink at 7.30, on my breakfast tray.

My G.P. came, examined me and said, 'She needs another course of antibiotics, Matron.' He said other things, as well. Helen must have come, too. But I can't remember seeing her that week. But I do remember saying, 'Please, Doctor, no more antibiotics. They make me feel like a very dead fish.'

Suddenly aware of all these pillows and his frequent visits, I said, 'Is this pneumonia, Doctor?'

'No,' he said, as if thinking aloud. 'But if you don't

take your other course of antibiotics, it soon will be.'

Then he told me I had a type of bronchitis. I can't remember the medical name he gave it. Today, Helen and my warm, lovely Nurse Vlast to see me for a little while.

I went on feeling like a dragon, breathing fire. And I longed for a strong, cool wind, straight from the open sea to blow over me. Then, one day, I was at last delivered of the virus. Once more, my increasingly perceptive G.P. said, 'Matron, she needs a holiday.' 'And a good deal more than that,' I could have added.

Thursday Yet another move is in the air. But where? And how soon? Tonight, hundreds of people like me must be stretching the midnight hours, trying to find a way to cope with this very same problem. Science, that so mercifully eases pain with one hand, with the other prolongs it to an utterly sterile, dead-end existence for too many. All you Nobel Prize winners, and you great research people at the Walter and Eliza Hall Institute, and elsewhere, why do you prolong life, if you don't make it worth living?

Friday Here's Helen. I'm minus two or three pillows and ready to enjoy visitors today.

Saturday Julie Shackleton and Barbara to see me for a while. Otherwise a very long day. At home I could be sitting in a comfortable chair, in a warm, light room with long windows on two sides that bring in the afternoon sun. And the silver birches.

Evening – Softly, my transistor is tuned to John Williams, his bewitching guitar, and Spain.

Suddenly a couple of doors away, above the music, the most compassionate and professional nurse who ever comes here, raises her voice as never before. Her patient is very deaf. She has a habit of protesting, especially at night, about no one knows what. To say she is thankless and aggressive is to praise her. Sister's voice again:

'Don't you dare bite me. If you do that again . . . ' she sounds desperate, 'I'll bite you back.'

Sometimes it's a struggle to prevent my deep love of people from turning to hate. This is one of the pains that all but one or two of my twenty odd neighbours will never know. For me, there's no escape from fearful nights like this. I wonder if the time will come when families and physicians can understand the torture of spirit that must be lived through in places like this. Something that flays the senses. It is pain that is deep-seated, and enduring. Different, but not less, than the pain of a scald, or a crushed or twisted limb. And it must happen to any man or woman when terminal illness sentences them to life in a so-called geriatric hospital alongside the mentally ill.

Too late now for John Williams. There's no sweet concord in music, broken as this has been tonight. There's much too much of this life-in-death nightmare. The climate that helps to make it grow and spread, I think, is segregation. Away from all people, places and things known and loved over the years. To keep my mind from crumbling I reach for *Dear Mama,* and surface tranquillity.

Gino arrived today.

Sunday Helen. Also Daisy and John with flowers, all of their own growing.

Monday Not very much worth-while remembering of things past this month. Except friends. And one's last look on things lovely.

Suddenly my door is pushed wide open. No knock or introduction. The voice tells me it must be the opulent old gentleman from the room opposite mine. He's very often audible on the telephone he's had installed. This he seems to use mainly to berate politicians and the police. Matron says he also owns a big refrigerator. This is beside his bed, to hold the contents of two cases. These I watch being delivered from a small van, parked just outside my window every week. That big square box that comes, fortnightly, is his supply of whisky. The longer, shallow case that comes every week, is filled with oysters and prawns. These are his steady diet. And vastly preferable they must be to the daily menu here. But, he tosses all their shells into his waste paper basket. Their aging, fishy smell grows hard to take as the day wears on. When my fastidious Helen comes, we always close the door as tightly as possible, but the reek of those stale shells still penetrates.

Without introduction, my uninvited guest stands in the wide open doorway and shouts at me:

'Your visitors have got a bloody cheek, coming into my room, day after day, and taking my chairs.'

Putting down my morning paper, perhaps foolishly, I reply, 'My visitors haven't taken your chairs. If anyone has taken them, it must be Matron or one of the nurses.'

Taking up the paper again, I add, 'My visitors wouldn't go *near* your room. I think you owe me an apology.' 'It's like their bloody cheek,' he persists. And so on. Then, like an angry turkey-cock, he struts away. Slipperless, without a gown, in tatty, old much-too-short pyjamas. He's fairly tall and gaunt, and makes a quaint scarecrow.

Back once more to the 'hatched, matched and despatched' column, as someone in the family used to call it. But no. The old fellow returns with an even mightier flow of language. Quite possibly he has 'oiled' it a little in the meantime.

This time, in lofty, after-dinner style, he shouts, 'And continuing my previous remarks... It's like their bloody cheek,' and so on.

I glance at the window and calmly go on reading, hoping it will slowly dawn on him that this blonde prefers gentlemen.

It's a pity. If he'd just been a shade different, this funny little episode could have ended with us both laughing over it, together. Poor old man. With all his whisky, prawns and oysters, he doesn't sound too happy.

This afternoon, that best of friends, Nurse Vlast comes to see me. Instead of sleeping, for she's on duty tonight at Prince Edward's, she toils out here by train and tram, across the river from one of the far western suburbs. She's big-hearted, and observant, always with a spice of humour. And much too generous with her violets and nougat.

It's hard to explain, but she sheds over me a kind of blessing. Something that stays with me long after she goes on her way, smiling, and larger than ever in her great winter coat.

Tuesday⃪ Helen to see me. I try to persuade her not to come so often. This is too forbidding, after all the light and warmth she leaves at home. It's utterly cheerless, with not even one comfortable chair to offer her.

Wednesday⃪ My sprightly social worker here again. She has sons of her own. Probably she has come to see that Gino is comfortably settled. And also to make sure that he can come in here and talk to me, occasionally. She is canny enough to see there is no possibility of any other communication for him here.

Darling Helen, this afternoon, better than her word, comes laden with a sack of bookshelves. They are modular, so that they can be re-arranged in various ways. Beautifully crafted, too, in dark brown wood that looks like black bean. They join perfectly, without aid of a single metal nail or screw. Very tiring for Helen, but she has made a perfect arrangement of the shelves. With them she brings books, my precious Renoir print, and a handful of winter rosebuds, too, with her own little bowl to hold them. Its glaze is the lovely, smoky green tint that some gumleaves have. There's a place for everything, books, prints, flowers, fruit – even a spot for Helen's ashtray. All these must be sun, moon and stars for me to steer by, and save my wits from foundering. Helen brings me happiness. It's only natural that it so often leaves with her.

Night falls early on Dawson Towers. Rain is playing on the tin roof of the toolshed just past my window. As if it is plucking the string of a guitar, at first... Now it's like a band of kettle-drums.

Thursday A gentle tap on my ever-open door. 'I'm Gino. May I come in?' It's a voice that makes you listen gladly. No accent whatever, but a slight musical intonation. His vowels have more colour than we give them.

'Come in, Gino. I've been expecting you.'

In his streamlined wheel-chair he propels himself quietly and quickly into the room. He has his wavy black hair like a man, is dark-eyed, and very fair-skinned. If he could stand he would be tall. If you could make him several pounds slimmer, and put him in doublet and hose, you would have one of Shakespeare's romantic, lute-strumming young gentlemen of Verona. You can see nature must have

97

had plans for Gino. Till hostile genes took over.

'Are you comfortable here?'

'Thank you. They are kind.' His face is as expressionless as a blank page of this diary. His too-calm expression tells me he already misses the warmth of an Italian household.

I offer him my little basket of fruit.

'Thank you. No.' He smiles. 'You see I have oranges.'

Perhaps someone in the family grows them. He does not say.

'Was it a car smash, Gino?'

'I have some obscure bone-disease.' He says it in a matter-of-fact way, as if he were telling me the day of the month.

'They don't know very much about it. I was fifteen when it happened.'

'Does it keep you in hospital all the time, like me?'

'Oh no. My mother always cares for me. I'm only here to give her a holiday.'

I wish his mother could see the light that for a moment transfigures him when he speaks of her, and just as quickly goes. He mentions that it will soon be lunchtime. Gino is going to miss his mother's minestrone and lasagne at Dawson Towers. It is exactly a quarter of an hour since he came into my room. I fancy he has politely timed this first visit.

'Thank you for coming to see me, Gino. Please come again.' Another of his rare smiles. Then he deftly backs his chair through my door and is gone. He will come back.

My G.P. to see me. He often comes about midday. The clinic is quite a distance from Dawson. If he has many patients to visit over this way, he can't have grace to eat his lunch, even. He looks me over and tells Matron I need a holiday. Matron herself goes into hospital for surgery in a couple of weeks. Without her, life would probably go on here. But for me it would be past bearing.

After the word 'holiday', the conversation, which they continue as they walk away from my bedside, is lost to me. Later Matron comes back and tells me my Doctor wants me to walk about as soon as ever I can.

Friday This afternoon Rose comes with more violets. Their scent has an elusive sweetness that's like no other flower I know. And as if they are not enough to stay me, she brings a most timely baby bottle of dry, delicious, ice-cold champagne, as well. There are just two things that make this way of living bearable – laughing a little, if you can, and better still, the enduring love of friends. So together, we laugh over ourselves when young, set the world to rights, and gossip happily about our families, as we do whenever we meet. My friends are far too dear for me to let the things that are shattering me burst through the seams while they are here.

Saturday Midmorning brings Gino. He stops near the bookshelves.

'You have books,' he says, with a lingering smile.

'Would you like to borrow one, Gino?'

'Thank you, no.' Again that attractive smile. He has 'many books'. Answering my question, he says he reads books about other countries, animals, especially animals, and what is going on in the world.

'Current history, Gino?'

'Yes, I wanted to be a lawyer. I would have been satisfied to be a teacher. But it could not be.' He hesitates. 'May I smoke?'

'Of course. Look, there's my sister's ashtray on the shelf beside you.'

I watch the well-kept hand take out a cigarette-case, then a cigarette and lighter. It is the left hand. His right hand seems to be almost useless. But the left does not falter.

Sunday⏴ Gino and our social worker, who seems to have him very much under her wing, come to see me this morning. In the afternoon he comes back again. Although he does not say a word about it, I'm certain he already feels the cold emptiness of this existence. But he has a very good friend who is married, with a home of his own. Sometimes, on a Saturday he will come here and drive him home to stay till Sunday afternoon.

Monday⏴ Helen is here with the first daffodils. They take me – body and soul. These Helen has brought are perfect. Gay tangerine cups with little fluted brims, and around them flawless, almost translucent pale yellow petals. Inside their cups there are fine golden stamens as a foil to all the sunlit yellows.

Tuesday⏴ Gino to see me. He *loves* animals. His great dane, Hero, goes everywhere with him when he is at home. I ask is Hero a one-man dog, or does he make friends with all the world? 'He is friendly. But,' says Gino, very decidedly, 'he is my dog.' He has a white rabbit too, and homing pigeons. They fly long distances, but they always come back to him, he says. He looks after all his little animal world himself. Exactly how he manages to do this I don't know. It must take a good deal of his limited energy, and plenty of patience and compromise, as well. He seems to have deep understanding and love of his happy living things. They are an extension of his family and friends.

'They live well,' he assures me. 'I do not give them

just anything. I feed them scientifically. They have their greens, their vitamins, and their minerals.' All this from a wheel-chair, with only one good hand, and the other a very lame one, to help him. Gino is showing me what even hemmed-in living can be, through his own magic casement.

Wednesday✶ Helen tells me when spring comes she is going for a week or so up the country to stay with Lucy.

Sister Mead comes today, and brings me rose-red camellias. She has driven miles to her home at Brighton to gather them and more miles across country to bring them here.

Thursday✶ Gino visits me this morning. He has a rare capacity for friendship. He doesn't seem to have visitors of his own. This makes me think all his friends are week-day students, or else are at work. But Gino would never think of himself as neglected. The nurses have not once mentioned him to me, although they must know we're acquainted.

My lovely, trusty Helen. And Ianthe too, with a feast of marvellous talk about the theatre. She makes me see just what she has seen. A marvellous gift – and her voice is music, as always. This is why she doesn't relish some of our brilliant new playwrights, who are very hard-pressed when it comes to finding the right word. And then putting it in the right place.

Saturday✶ Gino comes to tell me friends are coming after lunch to take him away for the night. They will bring him back tomorrow afternoon. He does not stay. He has 'to make preparations'.

In all this cold Kate and Sybil to see me. Kate's gifted granddaughter is going abroad to play with the Youth Orchestra. I fancy they said she is bound for Edinburgh.

Veronica, more than generous with the little time caring for her family and her other activities leave her, comes too, with her lovely Vanessa. Even in bulky woollens, Vanessa looks like a lost dryad in this place.

Today I walked a few steps.

Sunday Helen comes with Amanda who brings me one of her rare bouquets. Rare, because they all have the special beauty she can give them, and no two are ever alike. There are only three or four flowers – all that her garden has to offer today. But there are wonderful green and dull silver leaves, and one or two delightful, rather exotic sprigs that Amanda assures me she plucked from the vegetable garden.

These last two days have been really living. Nurse Sara is to walk me through the hospital. She takes me with some pride to see the two big wards at the front of the building. They look spotless, bright and airy and full of the wintry late afternoon sun that comes through very big bay windows facing west. They have ample curtains in a bold, happy design of bright, many-coloured flowers. The bedspreads repeat the colour of the flowers. This must be the part of the hospital that is inspected from time to time.

All the patients are fast asleep. I cannot think why, but this gentle nurse positively insists on taking me over to look, closely, at a bed in one corner. In this bed is a perfectly round form. The flesh is the colour of greyish clay. Only a matted cap of hair suggests that it is a woman. Small, and perhaps young, or maybe very old. The form looks exactly like the diagram of a foetus in a biology text-book. It has no interest for me. Just anguish that such things can be. My own room is drab and sordid compared with the wards. But I can't get back to it quickly enough.

Monday ♫ Woke towards morning with massive angina. Certain it was useless to ask that pretty night sister for an injection. At intervals I took three of the tablets that are always left beside me. And held out till Matron came on duty in the early morning. She was good to me, and so deft. Helen to see me. A very lazy day.

Tuesday ♫ Gino to see me. He looks very serious today.

'You do not mind?' he says, feeling for his cigarette-case and lighter. He takes one draw. Then he speaks, after a pause.

'I would like to marry.'

'That's very natural, Gino.'

Another silence.

'I would not marry a virgin.'

'Why not, Gino?'

As if thinking aloud, he says very slowly, 'Because I could not give her all a husband should.'

Another of those silences.

'But I would be very good to her,' he says softly and firmly.

'I know you would, Gino.'

'My parents will find someone. A widow. She will not miss what I cannot give.'

He is a man, indeed, in intelligence. And yet with it, he still has the frankness and something of the endearing simplicity of childhood.

Now he has said what he really came to tell me. Another cigarette, and he goes unusually quickly on his way.

I lie back and think long thoughts about Gino. He's sensitive and can understand and even share in the thoughts and feelings of other people. Yet he would never dream of crossing the threshold of anyone's holy of holies. He holds himself in hand always, one can see, on a pretty tight rein. With sadness I often think how dearly he must have bought all this calm and touching wisdom. The price, paid in full, is the red, sweet wine of youth. It could be that this is what he has been telling me today.

Tuesday Monday ended in yet another of Those Nights. Angina. And all that goes with it. My one and only Helen comes. No one else could bear me. Morphine never gives me those fabulous trips some poets and other writers talk about. It doesn't even give me good sound sleep. Perhaps pain doesn't let it.

Wednesday Gino to see me. I ask him how he fills in the long days when he is at home. Well, he has his car. He explains he has had it properly fitted to give him complete control when he is driving.

'Do you drive all round your neighbourhood to meet your friends and acquaintances, Gino?'

'Not always.' He smiles.

Sometimes he goes into the country, he tells me, to see his sister. Fifty miles there and fifty miles back. His wheel-chair fits in the car. Hero goes with him too. Sometimes he buys lunch on the way.

'You don't tell your mother about these long drives, do you, Gino?'

'No.' Again that quiet smile.

'You don't tell her because she would worry about you.'

'That is the reason,' he replies, faintly amused.

On one of my bookshelves he notices the little bowl filled with the lovely, very early primroses Helen brought me yesterday. Evidently, they give him pleasure, too.

'They are like champagne,' he says.

'Primroses, Gino. Don't you know them?'

No, he doesn't think he has ever seen them before. 'I must go,' he says. 'Not to tire you.'

He leaves just in time. My G.P. arrives a few minutes later. He did say a holiday. But that may have been the persuasive carrot to get me on to my feet again. He wants me to walk. I would. I would gladly make the despairing effort, if he could show me a little path, here, no matter how narrow, that is a green and pleasant place to walk in.

'There's a room vacant in a rest home,' my G.P. says, 'some distance from here. I want you to look at it.' He's doing his best for me. Useless to say that I don't want to look at any nursing home or rest home, ever again. I want to look at the open sky and white gums and violet-misted everlasting hills. I want to stand and watch white-crested breakers crashing on to rocks with the soft wind blowing over me from the sea. Can't he understand?

'Your sister knows all about it. She will take you there.'

'Thank you, Doctor. I'll go.' I haven't the courage to tell him to be very careful this time. He'd never understand that out of all the months in both the nursing homes he's already put me, there has not been one single instant that anyone could want to make eternity.

'Do you think she could manage it the day after tomorrow, Matron?'

Yes. It can be managed. Another plan for my disposal. I only wish I could feel more gracious. No one should lay hands on someone else's life. Though this time, at least, they let me say 'yea' or 'nay'. Or, do they? If I had had one look inside this room beforehand, no tow-truck could ever have dragged me here.

Gino is my only visitor today.

After lunch, determined to make my legs, as well as my mind, consent to Friday's outing, I walk up the corridor. The lounge can't be avoided. Along the two walls, facing each other, are the same tight rows of unsmiling strangers. No one ever admits that the other exists. There's no communication whatever.

No human being wants to be regimented. Some small part of every man and woman longs to be treated as a person. That is the everlasting need behind these masks in the lounge. Old people don't look for gifts. They want visits from family and friends. Their need is to be cared for, too, not in isolation, but in some way not too painfully remote from the kind of surroundings where they have spent most of their lives.

Anonymous help is grand for raising buildings and equipping them, but what is impersonal never can be more than cold comfort.

To care for old people calls for warm perception, patience and special skills. And not in these stark, disciplined lounges, but in some room where they can move about like human beings, where there is sunlight and fresh air, where sometimes they can listen to music, with nostalgic melody and rhythm that can bring back the happy light of other days. A single picture on one of these grim walls could open windows on another world.

Men and women with terminal illness may have hardened arteries and creaking joints, but their minds are in no way crippled. For them to be enclosed in nursing homes where night and day, senility, with its apathy, strident garrulity, and frequently painful psychiatric problems, must call the tune for everyone, can only be a living death.

This is not my day for walking that can only be in

this one direction.

Back in my room a cold sense of nothingness takes hold of me. Nothingness that has sinister tendrils. Not tendrils – tentacles that spread, and pierce. For the first time I've begun to be afraid it will drain away that essential me that I'm fighting to keep alive. After all this meaningless expense of spirit, how can you ever again be the human being you once hoped you were? If you are lucky, you may come out of it as seasoned timber. But, buried too soon, even tall trees can become as fossilized as coal. And no way near as useful.

Flicking over the pages of this book of bits and pieces, I find copied in pencil, on the last leaf: 'I have a very simple creed: that life and joy and beauty are better than dusty death.' – Bertrand Russell (aet. 90). Only two years before he wrote this the Establishment had sent Bertrand to prison for his part in a civil disobedience strike against nuclear warfare.

Another night jagged with hideous sounds. No book is anodyne for this. Pity and thinking take you nowhere, either. Somewhere a clock strikes two. Pain. Dark, tight pain. A fiend bears down on my chest with a load of mischief that spills through my arm down to its very finger tips. I wish someone would come...

Thursday At last. Someone did come. A prick. Then slowly – forgetfulness. Sometimes after pain, not immediately, but the next day, I'm curiously aware. Everything seems sharp-edged, bright and clear – perhaps a little too clear. Helen comes bringing slacks, woollen jacket and big tweed coat to fit me out for tomorrow's excursion. Our destination is Vere de Vere House, four or five miles from here. But Helen knows the way.

August

Friday The car is as warm as a spring day. The window beside me is even faintly sunlit. Prickling with expectation I set out. It's like it used to be, waiting with bated breath, for the curtain to rise on the transformation scene. I really don't mind if we never get there. The trees along the road are green. In the gardens early wattle, camellias, daffodils, and bright ribbons of polyanthus primulas are all in flower. There's even something spectacular about a couple of black spaniels sniffing at strange fences.

Vere de Vere House is on a corner. Square and solid, with a big bay window and two verandahs. The one facing west looks on to lawn, a sheltering, but not dense hedge, and two or three shrubs. The house is red brick, about 1900 vintage. So is the door-bell. In the hall there are fresh flowers. The Matron very briskly shows me the room which is just inside the front door. It is very big and made bright by two windows that take up most of one wall. Wherever we walk is emerald green carpet, mottled with peacock blue. The bed, which has a cover to match, looks like a doll's bed. This is because the room is so big, and because there is no dressing-table, or any small table where one could put a T.V. set, or write a letter. Two very small chairs with seats covered in dark-blue vinyl, have skeleton backs all metal, that look like exclamation marks. On one wall there has once been a vast, deep, open fireplace. This has been built in to make a more than adequate hanging wardrobe, with a full-length mirror on the inside of the door. The recesses beside it have become two cupboards, each about five feet high, very deep, and divided by a single shelf. They would be ideal for storing golf-clubs or any other sporting gear, and of course, suitcases, in quantity. Both are pretty hopeless for clothes. Beside the bed there's a small locker with three shallow drawers. Its top holds a water-jug and a metal lamp, curved like a hooded cobra about to spring. There are lacy nylon curtains to the windows. But, it is all freshly painted white and looks spotless.

We ask if we may see the bathroom. It is incredibly small for its very big bath, toilet, and basin. But they all fit in, as well as the smallest shower recess I've ever seen. Everything sparkles with cleanliness.

Yes, Matron will give injections, as necessary. Breakfast is served in bed. But if her Ladies should need bed-rest, they must go straight to hospital. My allergy to milk and its products is mentioned. No comment on this whatever. Matron is young, graceful and very becomingly dressed in tone with her attractive colouring. She also is tight-lipped.

We are left to ourselves for a few minutes for me to make up my mind. The fees compare with a good motel, without any of the amenities. But, it is clean, airy and seems peaceful. Well rugged up in top coats we are both freezing. But Helen is certain there will be some kind of heating turned on when I move in. In any case it should be a delightful room in a hot summer. And there's a green lawn and hedge outside. So I decide to take the room, thank Matron for showing it to us, and arrange to come in on Monday afternoon.

Saturday Gino is off for the week-end which makes me happy. It is good to have known him. There will be no one here for him to talk to now. But his parents and brother will be home, he says, in a few weeks. I think we both part with regret.

This week the media have made something of a stir over old age pensioners living together, without benefit of clergy. Bless them. In this way they are cutting exactly in half their expenses for electricity, gas for cooking, rent, and so are putting up some slight resistance to the pressures all round them. But, they are also laying themselves open to a witch-hunt. For some devious reason the pension rate for a married couple is reduced to less than the combined rate of two single pensioners. Does a warm coat or a pair of shoes, or even a loaf of bread cost you less if you are married, than if you are single? Besides, there's no compassion in this too-complacent view that sex at seventy is indecent. Our betters, backed by history and science, tell us that it is not only possible, in many instances it is good for man and woman. The biological urge is not a thing that anyone can computerize. And so far there doesn't seem to have been very much research on the date-line when there can be no intercourse except from soul to soul. Even at seventy plus, your private life should be your own, provided you do not hurt anyone. Which doesn't seem a bad thought to leave behind me at Dawson Towers.

VERE DE VERE HOUSE

Monday ◢ At three o'clock, as requested, we arrive at Vere de Vere House. Matron opens the door, picks up one suitcase and takes it into my room.

'Tea is at five,' she says and leaves us to unpack.

This morning's temperature was 5°C and is probably only two or three degrees higher now. Helen finds a power-point, but there is no sign of a radiator. She takes my electric blanket out of its box, and turns back the bed covers to put it in its place, then realises she needs help to lift that good heavy mattress and adjust the tapes. 'This room is absolutely perishing,' she says, still buttoned up in a coat and scarf, as I am, too. 'I'll have to get help with this blanket.' It is some little time before she manages to make contact. She comes back with Matron, who eyes the blanket with distaste. But she helps Helen put it in place and re-make my bed.

'Matron, we've found the power-point, but there doesn't seem to be a radiator in here. Will you give me one, please?' I dare to ask.

'There is no radiator for this room.'

Helen, with that enchanting smile of hers, quickly takes over.

'Never mind, Matron, my sister has her own radiator. I'll slip over with it early tomorrow morning.' But –

'I do not allow radiators in my Ladies' rooms. They are too dangerous.' Helen and I look at each other and smile. We are both freezing, still buttoned-up in our coats and scarves. And my two suitcases are still unpacked. But just what escape is there for me, *anywhere*?

'There is a heater in the lounge,' says Matron, then departs.

'"The ice was here, The ice was there, The ice was all around," – in more ways than one,' I murmur to Helen.

Still it is clean. And there are no searing cries. So we unpack and stow away my belongings as best we can. Helen leaves me, but promises to come back early tomorrow afternoon.

The lounge is also the diningroom. Tonight the evening meal is three sticks of pencil-thin asparagus on a square of toast. There are also ample servings of a solid-looking milk pudding, with cream. There is no substitute for me, but there is one slice of bread for everyone, and butter and jam to go with it, on the table that is completely covered with all-over synthetic lace. My seat is at the end facing the kitchen door. There are two doors into this lounge-diningroom, as well as a wide-open archway opening on to what I imagine are other bedrooms. There is a space-heater at the far end of the room, half on, 'so that the room will not get overheated'. Matron waits at table. On my left is a charming, very old lady, Mrs Dermott-Smith. On my right two characters who do not speak. Nor do they, unless asked, pass anything this very big table holds, to anyone sitting near them. Five chairs with ample cushioned seats and backs of blue corduroy are ranged on blue-green carpet along one wall. Their bare, wooden arms all touch each other, like sardines in a tin. You are allotted one of these chairs, just as you are given your desk at school. The chairs are not uncomfortable, but any casual grouping is forbidden. And easy, informal talk is discouraged. My chair is between Mrs Simpson and Miss Joskin, my right-hand neighbours at table.

The meal is soon over and all ladies retire to their chairs. The table is cleared and there is silence, again like boarding-school. At half-past six the television set is officially turned on. This is especially for Mrs Dermott-Smith. There's a football replay, and she is a keen follower of the game. The T.V. blinks and stutters for several minutes.

'I don't think it's quite tuned to the station,' I venture. And being the most alert and able-bodied of the Ladies present, I move towards the set.

'Oh no,' comes a chorus, '*no* one is allowed to touch the T.V.' Whereupon, Mrs Dermott-Smith, whose corner seat is almost on top of the set, leans forward and quickly makes the necessary adjustment. The news session follows.

By eight o'clock Matron appears. On the wall opposite me is a large coloured print in blues and greens, to match the carpet. Above what must be a big fireplace, now partly hidden by our space-heater, is the twin of this misty landscape, with a slight difference. The colouring is the same. In other respects it is a poor relation of Landseer's *Dying Stag*. From colour schemes and art, my mind is wrenched back to the facts of life. There is a general movement, and without a word being spoken, it is subtly conveyed to me that Ladies are expected to retire at eight o'clock.

There is no hot drink by way of supper. So I take my thermos, knock on the kitchen door, and ask if I may have it filled with boiling water, explaining a hot drink has been prescribed for me with my night issue of pills. The thermos is brought to my room later, by someone who is a relative of Matron's, and is also our cook-housekeeper. She seems a pleasant woman. But no, she couldn't possibly give me a cup and saucer and spoon. 'They are all needed.'

'Perhaps a glass then.' Eventually a glass arrives. It is thick and heavy and there is no possible chance of its breaking, if I give it a little warming first. I've switched the electric blanket on, but everything around is so cold it will be some time before the bed is really warm. Shivering, I find something to read, and hopefully pull the bed's two not very lavish blankets over me. From my pillows, I'm very conscious of a vase on the cupboard nearest the door. It is filled with paper imitations of four big pink roses. They are very well made. But I would much prefer to have them inside that cupboard. Instead, I decide that in the morning I will be diplomatic and simply push them back as far beyond my line of vision as possible. It may be odd, but paper flowers always speak to me of dust and ashes.

A couple of hours later, warm at last, and desperately tired, I open my thermos. It holds a scant cup of lukewarm water. It probably never was boiling. To hold the heat for several hours, most people know a thermos must be filled. How to melt Helen's chicken cubes, without even a spoon to stir them, is a problem. Suddenly I remember the versatile little fruit knife that was given me as a souvenir of the second Elizabeth's coronation. I manage to unearth it, and it performs well. But my night cap is very nearly stone-cold.

'If you should ever be ill at night be sure you ring for Matron, darling,' were Helen's parting words. There is no bell.

Tuesday ☞ I gaze at the small birds darting in and

out of the pittosporum hedge that is hesitating into flower. They are already beginning their biological control of the insects that will soon relish three double rows of seedling stocks and Iceland poppies planted in the bed outside my window. The hedge hides me and my bed from the street, but lets me see both street and trees, and the big sunlit house on the opposite corner.

An antiquated white truck with a load of bri-quettes shaves the corner. Ten minutes later it comes back with the same hairbreadth technique. I smile at the idea that this simple everyday going and coming should seem like an ·event. One of the effects, I suppose, of segregation. Eight o'clock. Breakfast: a genteel little tray with a slice of hot-buttered toast and a pot of tea. I supplement it with one of Helen's navel oranges. Early morning is not my most bril-liant hour. Besides, bed is warm, and the rest of the room is still icy. It is well after nine when I amble towards the shower. When I return to my room Matron has just finished making my bed. In words that fall like chips of ice she says, 'I want you to be out of the bathroom, *always,* before half-past nine, Miss Newton, so that I can shower my Ladies.' Well. There is a second bathroom. And she obviously can't be 'showering' her sundry Ladies in both at the same time. Her problem must surely be the very tempera-mental hot water service which has just frozen and frizzled me by turns. Too meekly, I reply, 'Very well, Matron'. Trailing her little, brief authority, she departs.

Afternoon tea is around half-past two, and with it comes Helen. The Ladies sit in serried rank with little tables and their tea-trays touching their knees. Mrs Baxter, our housekeeper, very kindly brings an extra cup for Helen. After tea, we withdraw to my room, which, even in our warmest coats, we both find incredibly cold. The early morning temperature was 5°C. It must have risen since then, but only in a very modest way.

'Apart from the cold, how are things?' Helen asks.

'I think I've been told most of the rules. Ill or well, out of the bathroom by 9.30 a.m. Chairs are all allotted, and must not be moved out an inch from the wall. I haven't been told that "Ladies are not allowed to entertain Gentlemen in their rooms" yet, but I dare say that will come, if Dick and David should visit me.' For the first time this afternoon, Helen smiles. Unwillingly, I mention that I could do with a cup, saucer and spoon, which she finds surprising.

So we drive home and bring back with us the pretty china that David gave me as a Christmas gift plus one teaspoon. Helen is slim and no great height, but she has remarkable dignity. With both in evidence, and a light in her eye, she insists on taking the crockery to the kitchen herself. She is not long away. We have a good laugh over the ways of the world in this genteel rest home. Its mystique is a wide open field for any behavioural scientist. Another cigarette and Helen leaves me, promising to come again tomorrow and take me shopping.

Wednesday We go shopping and come back with garments, if not exactly apres-ski, certainly woollier and heavier than I've ever owned in my life.

Today has been an entertainment, especially the crowds of people of all ages, shapes and sizes. Skirts have retracted thighwards again since my last outing. All the strident sounds of living, even loud-speakers, above the talk and laughter of the streets, were not in the least disturbing. Fascinated, sitting beside Helen,

I watched overcrowded trams cut harmless swathes through the double lines of cars.

Thursday At last a morning paper: presumably the one ordered by request last Monday. In the meantime, but rather late in the day, Mrs Dermott-Smith has lent me hers. Struggling painfully, on two satin-surfaced, stout blackwood sticks, she manages to walk unaided from her room to her corner seat in the lounge every day. She may have her ninetieth birthday early next year they tell me. She still has the faded vestiges of beauty, is tall and slender, and even now has the rare autumnal grace of some of the women Sargent painted. She's very quick on the uptake, and her charm and warmth make her good company, though she is rather deaf. Wound in her mohair rug she sits and reads, till she falls asleep. In waking hours, she crochets a gay little cover for a cradle, and the child she probably will not see.

Miss Joskin is already in her seat that touches my left elbow. There is a sixth chair against the wall opposite. It is always kept vacant probably in case Matron wishes to use it, which so far she has not. It is never offered to a visitor. Visitors are in no way encouraged. I open my paper and Miss Joskin immediately asks me to read her the finance pages, as she cannot see. Her sight is failing, but it might be improved by glasses, which she does not possess. She seems to have no difficulty in pointing out to me the headlines of any items that concern her. No news except finance is of the least interest. Matron has already informed me that Miss Joskin is an exceedingly wealthy lady, and has her own secretary who comes here once or twice a week to do her bidding. Miss Joskin came to Vere de Vere House from hospital. Before that she lived entirely alone, in a big antiquated house in an outer suburb. It has no heating or hot water service, and from Matron's description, plumbing and lighting of about the same year as Federation. She sounds like yet another of those rich, elderly women who live alone and suffer from severe malnutrition.

I fancy Matron has given me these uninvited bio-graphical details as barter for Helen's and my own family-tree. If any. Startling revelations that she seems to be waiting for, are not likely to be forth-coming from me.

Mrs Dermott-Smith is Matron's status symbol. Mrs Simpson has been out to lunch with friends. Nobody here ever talks to her except Matron and Mrs Baxter – both very buoyant personalities. In their own fashion they are probably kind, and may understand her. To all my attempts to interest Mrs Simpson she says, just like a talking doll, 'Yes', 'No', 'Thank you', 'I miss my family', as she continues to gaze into space. It's pitiful that nothing's being done to give her the smallest motivation. She's middle-aged, well-preser-ved, and seems physically very strong. Though a widow, she looks as if she has enjoyed all the good things of life. Her friends often call and take her out, and her son and his wife and children are devoted to her. Every night since I have been here she takes a shower at two a.m., and another at four, in the bathroom next door to me. At first I thought the sounds that wakened me were rain. But she leaves all doors wide open, and through my door I can see the blaze from two hall lights and the bathroom.

Saturday☞ No visitors today for me.

Sunday☞ This morning I walk round the block.

Monday☞ Last night, angina. Matron was in her room opposite, looking at television with her door firmly closed. I called once but naturally she couldn't hear me. I did my best with sub-lingual tablets, without much effect. Then I remembered brandy sometimes helped. The pain has been worse, and at last, I slept. That one gentle stroll into the world surely can't have had anything to do with this bout of pain. But maybe the intense cold of the room has. Yesterday, as I came from my triumphant stroll Matron followed me into my room.

'Miss Newton, you have no *right* whatever to go walking in those light shoes. It's much too dangerous.' The delinquents are my favourite black suede court shoes. 'You must get proper *flat-heeled* shoes if you want to go out walking.'

Heaven forbid that one of her Ladies should burden this practical matron with the care of a sprained ankle. But possibly she's right.

'Perhaps I'll look for some walking shoes when I'm out this afternoon, Matron.'

Helen comes early and brings the little old English brass bell that has been on my bedside table at home for the last few years. We then speed off to Chadstone to buy those compulsory shoes, also some even more necessary provisions. The shoes we manage to find are not in the least unsightly. They are displayed, and approved by the establishment. To be quite honest, Matron has a *flair* for clothes. These different 'jet-set' outfits she wears, day after day, may not be all vanity. I fancy she has an extra sense for dress and uses it as a kind of fulfilment, like a musician with violin or oboe or a painter with palette and brushes. The difference is that Matron can't communicate. An artist does. It's not easy to take all her insensitive rules and regulations. And hardest of all is the pseudo-gentility, unless you can laugh at it. If a cat were allowed at Vere de Vere House, which it is not, it would have to be at least a pedigreed Siamese or chinchilla. Humour and compassion go hand in hand. A dash of either would add considerably to the gaiety of this little rest home.

Tuesday∅ Miss Joskin sits waiting for me and my morning paper. I go through the daily drill of annual meetings and stock exchange quotations of selected gilt-edged shares. Some of her shares have made a very substantial rise. 'I've got six thousand of them,' she says and smacks her lips. When the money-market has been dealt with, Miss Joskin, already in top-coat and bucket-shaped felt hat, muffled to the chin, belts off for her daily walk. She's a plump little old-fashioned type who is afraid of everything. As if she's had a narrow, frustrated childhood, and has never been able to find her way out of it. She makes you feel she has nothing whatever in her life to look back on with a laugh, or even with the amused, happy sigh many people have for things past. Her only reasons for living seem to be her money, her health and her food. Nearly everything that comes to the table, she protests, disagrees with her. However, she eats all that is offered to the very last crumb, without any visible ill-effects.

Wednesday∅ Already in my top-coat like most of the others, the sunlight, pale and thin though it is, draws me into the garden. There's a frail, young magnolia, with one flower just open, and a bud to follow. Facing due west, outlining the big bay windows of Matron's quarters, there's a wide bed of flowering native shrubs. A boronia is already in bud, but it will take much warmer sun than this to induce its green and brown petals to unfold.

After a turn or two along the curving path that

separates flower-beds from lawn, Mrs Baxter joins me. She and Matron do the housework between them, with the help of a very pleasant girl from southern Europe who is here most mornings until lunch. Mrs Baxter takes great interest in this newly-made garden, and in the keen old gardener who is working in it today. The garden is her love, rather than its flowers. She likes to put a plant in the ground, to water it and watch it grow. It is the height and thickness of her trellis of sweet peas that count. The colour and shape and scent of their early flowers don't seem to give her much joy. Soon she leaves me to attend to our midday meal. It is no secret that Mrs Baxter sees herself as a cordon bleu. Her deep freeze cuisine as it reaches our table reminds me of Jenny's when she was doing junior domestic science at her country high school. It may be that good-natured Mrs Baxter's real expertise finds itself in opening tins and cartons.

From the front gate I discover there are at least four good level blocks for walking to the right, and probably eight to ten, equally inviting blocks, to the left. The garden is enjoyable where there is sun. But with no hills to stop me, I'm all for walking abroad. Five minutes the first day, ten minutes the next, fifteen minutes the day after, and so on to a good solid half-hour. Today my plan for survival is made. It might even turn out to be a stratagem for escape.

This could be a happy place. A Miss Ann Laurie is permanently seated between Mrs Dermott-Smith and Miss Joskin. Like her namesake her voice is low and sweet, and her English woos the ear with a charming, very faint Scots burr. She has been bonnie, too, with a small, well-poised head of soft, smooth, iron-grey curls. Beside Miss Joskin she looks like someone strayed out of *Sense and Sensibility* into the earthy world of Charles Dickens. Much travel and the background of a pioneer cattle family give her many interests. She is crippled by arthritis. But her mind needs no crutch, except on odd days when her memory deserts her completely for a short while. On these occasions she takes me as a partner in her daily crossword.

Once more, enduring Helen has insisted on re-erecting my shelves. Kate and Sybil to see me this afternoon with camellias and heavenly scented viburnum from their garden, David Niven's *The Moon is a Balloon*, and Gavin Maxwell's fascinating *Ring of Bright Water*, that I couldn't fully enjoy the first time they lent it to me.

Friday ☞ August is nearly over. One couldn't feel at home here. Still, one month has gone. With Helen it's possible to live a little outside four walls, and to enjoy seeing my friends without their having to endure the cold and discomfort of my quarters.

Mrs Dermott-Smith has visitors. She has no immediate family but from time to time come her 'greats', and 'great-greats', with two coveys of delightful, golden-haired, very young children who are not in the least abashed by the array of old ladies lining the wall. Very slowly, from attractive bits and pieces and without any patterns, she puts together such ingenious and amusing dolls, and quaint, small soft animals to entertain this growing clan.

Except for the occasional full-stop for angina, and two or three very wet days, my walks abroad are a growing delight. There's just one thing that almost turns my plans to emptiness and sends me back to the house much sooner than need be. This is unhappy, impenetrable Mrs Simpson.

September

Thursday Today, no sooner am I seen with coat, gloves and stick than Mrs Baxter, who evidently is in charge of Mrs Simpson while Matron showers the other Ladies, stops me, as usual.

'Oh, you *would* like to take Mrs Simpson with you, wouldn't you?' And, 'Oh, aren't you going to take Mrs Simpson with you today?' She has her formula ready. I can't bring myself to say no. But the motive in giving me this millstone, day after day, is hard to find – except that a woman of her strong build must need outdoor exercise more than the rest of us. Yet, so far, I've not even seen her take a turn around the garden. After several days of compulsory outings, she is still as impassive as the footpath we are treading. There is no sign that she's even aware she's out of doors. As we go past rows of small, well kept houses, she doesn't glance at one sunlit garden. And some are already alive with the colours of early spring. Man, beast, bird, flower, I've tried them all. Nothing brings the slightest response. How can it be pleasure for her? For me it is like walking beside a hearse.

Friday Helen is away now, for a well earned holiday, in the Riverina with Lucy.

Today Naomi came to see me and brought me twelve fabulous oranges. They lit up the lounge, as if they were big, golden lamps. She and Alec bought them on their drive home from Adelaide, somewhere near Mildura. It was generous of her to remember me so handsomely, for I've really never seen their like. The only place where we could sit together and talk, was side by side on two hard, stiff chairs at the dining-table. Rather like Punch and Judy with the Ladies in their straight row of chairs opposite for audience.

After Naomi left me, I offered the Ladies my oranges. Mrs Simpson accepted one, like a polite sleep-walker. Strangely, life hasn't written one single line of worry, joy, or grief upon her face. The sadness of it. Each of the others took one with a smile that had in it a gentle shock of surprise and pleasure. It was touching to see that look of happiness over so small a thing.

The Sunday before Helen left for the country she took me home with her to have lunch with a couple of other guests. Everything was perfectly arranged. But for me it was bitter-sweet. I'm not sure that I can go home again.

Saturday Today, Rose came with Amanda and took me to afternoon tea at an amusing little coffee lounge, with very good coffee, in Toorak. Its walls are covered with small oils, one or two abstracts, but mostly landscape and still-life. I didn't notice any budding Nolans or Dobells among them, but they were gay and decorative – and young.

Sunday I think Helen must have told all my friends she was going to be out of town, and that's why I'm enjoying so many visitors. Today Ruth is calling to take me home to afternoon tea with her and Joseph. Their flat, with its fine view of the skyline will be swimming in sunlight this early spring day, and Joseph may put on a record of Topol's for us.

Tuesday Soon after I'm in bed Matron comes into my room. She has been shopping at her 'special' boutique and now she is 'not sure about it'. Guessing the reason for her call I ask if she would like to show me the frock she has bought. Yes. She thinks she would. After a little time she comes back wearing the dress, its long skirt furling and flowing like reeds in gently moving water. The sleeves are long and close-fitting and the bodice back is high. The front dips in a wide open V, revealing but discreet, to meet a white peony at her waist. But for that touch of ice she could be beautiful. Opening my wardrobe door, she studies herself in the long mirror. Then, at last, she says, 'I think it needs something.'

'A tiara, perhaps?' I long to suggest. Instead, with all the truth that's in me at the moment, I say 'It's elegant and you wear it beautifully, Matron. It could have been especially designed for you.'

'Perhaps,' she says with a glittering smile. To-night, Matron, the strong one who seems to find pleasure in manipulating her Ladies, has shown me that she is basically insecure. All these fine feathers, and they really are fine, could be compensation for frustration in depth. She must be driven by some sinister urge not to let any of her Ladies move those regimented chairs one inch. The same force makes her insist that I continue to freeze, rather than let me use my own radiator in my icy room for an hour or two a day.

Wednesday Last night I nearly froze. It was a relentless cold crouching over me. The electric blanket was switched to three, yet I kept waking to sheets that hadn't even lost their first, unused chill. With morning, the blanket was out of order. It has not had much use. But several times at Vere de Vere House I did notice bed-makers drag roughly at the switch for no apparent reason. There doesn't seem much to be done about it until Helen comes home. And Veronica, who so quickly fixes the thought to the deed, happens to be unexpectedly away for a few days, too.

As usual Matron is in my room when I come in

from the shower. She hears about my minor tragedy with complete unconcern. 'Perhaps you could lend me a hot water bag until I can do something about the blanket, Matron?'

'I do not have hot water bags here,' she says very quickly. Nor does she offer me a rug or an extra blanket of the ordinary kind. The temperature was 3°C early this morning. Possibly Matron does not feel the cold. But she always puts a very efficient radiator, which runs from a point inside her rooms, in the hall exactly opposite my door on the mornings my G.P. comes to see me. As soon as he leaves, it is returned to its permanent habitat. Of course, I could walk towards the shopping centre, and keep walking, till I find a chemist, and buy a hot water bag. But though I've experienced nothing that could be wildly called the warmth of hospitality since I've been here, for some possibly quixotic reason, I can't bring myself to defy this peculiar, vulnerable woman under her own roof.

This morning there are signs of rain. Already equipped for her walk, Miss Joskin decides to take her exercise in the hall. Within seconds she is beside me again.

'Not allowed to walk in the hall.' Grunt. 'She says it will wear out the carpet.' Another grunt. Then, 'Do you know Matron is married?'

'No, Miss Joskin.'

'No one here has ever seen the husband. There's a child, too, at school.'

What Miss Joskin would plainly like this dull morning is a good, cosy gossip over the front fence. Seeing my talent doesn't lie that way she returns to the weather.

'I do hope it doesn't rain this afternoon. Miss

Harvey is coming and it's a long walk for her back the station.'

'You could ring for a taxi for her,' I suggest.

'Oh no,' this with meaningful finality, 'I couldn't do *that*.'

Thursday It seems to me that outdoor exercise has been prescribed for Mrs Simpson and that day by day, I'm to be the one to give it. This morning, when we've walked in utter silence several blocks from the house, suddenly she says,

'How could you get to town from here?'

Even to hear the toneless sound of her voice amazes me. I suggest a taxi. There must be a train and tram somewhere, too. But I try to explain to her that I've no idea where they are, as I've never been anywhere, except by car, in this neighbourhood. Silence follows. She has no further questions whatever. Nor is there the least sign that she has understood me.

Tonight, I put back on my bed the heavy chenille quilt that is always removed at night, and carefully folded away. On top of this are my tweed coat and two heavy woollen jackets.

The fifth test match, having been put forward by bad weather, is coming to us by satellite this week. There are probably plenty of far worse fools than 'the flannelled fools at the wicket', but I don't lose any sleep over them, or the run-stealers. Our unpredictable Matron has announced that she is staying up every night till stumps to watch the game.

Matron insists on tinkering with my T.V. set for nearly half an hour, with scraps of wire, hair clips and plastic clothes pegs to produce an aerial that will bring me a steady image. About the cricket, I couldn't care less. But it would be a change, for once, to have a good play, some interview in depth, or an outdoor documentary. At last an image. It is gone as Matron passes through my door in triumph, and does not return.

Friday A fine day though far from sunny. With Mrs Simpson by my side, to break the deadliness of the exercise, we walk in a new direction. We pass a wide fence with cascades of mauve wisteria shedding its elusive scent all round us. It looks as if a shopping-centre could be the full stop to this very long street. We come to a corner shop where they have oranges and Granny Smith apples, soup cubes, biscuits and sweets among other things I need to stay me in the cold, hungry hours between my scanty evening meal and breakfast. As we step inside, Mrs Simpson at last speaks. She would like to buy sweets for her grand-children. This proves a. drawn-out undertaking. Knowing exactly what my needs are, my shopping is soon over. Turning to put fruit and other odds and ends in my basket, I'm dismayed to find my charge has noiselessly slipped away from my side, unseen by the shopkeeper or by me. I hurry outside. There is no sign of her in any direction. She has her handbag with her and may have wandered round the corner into the shopping centre. For at least a quarter of an hour I hurry in and out of any shops that may have taken her fancy, enquiring if anyone has seen her. She is a tall woman, striking in a strange way, and would probably be remembered. No one has caught sight of the woman I describe. Then back again to the corner shop in case she has come back there to look for me. No sign. Desperate, I stand looking up to-wards the crowded main road and across it at what could be the entrance to a railway station. It is near lunch-time, and being Friday there is an endless chain of traffic. Two double lines of cars and the occasional heavy truck are speeding north and south. For an instant they slow down a little. And there, in the midst of that milling crowd, like a figure carved in stone, stands Mrs Simpson. I can't say how I managed to get to her through the cars, take her arm and calmly bring her back to the footpath. Because quite simply, I'll never know. And I've neither nerve nor skill in coping with traffic. On the way back shortness of breath must have made my complete silence match Mrs Simpson's. Fear that she might have been hurt had drained every last drop of energy from me. I wasn't even sure that she would tell anyone who found her who she was or where she lived. Or even if she could tell them. Our walk had been much longer than usual. When I told Mrs Baxter the drama that had caused the delay, her incredible reaction was, 'Just fancy that!' Not one other word.

Saturday This morning there was the usual, 'Aren't you taking Mrs Simpson with you, Miss Newton?'

'No. Not in her present mood, Mrs Baxter.'

There was no reply. But from today I walk alone, or not at all. A listless ray of sun reaches almost to the symmetrical, alternate curves of Iceland poppy and stock seedlings. Suddenly, I know I must walk. I must not be here when those seedlings flower.

October

Sunday In four days Helen will be home. It is almost like summer today. The garden is swimming in golden light. Already Mrs Simpson has gone off for the day with her family and will not return till bedtime. I'm going to enjoy myself in the garden with a book. But, no. Matron decides she will take her Ladies for a drive this afternoon. I protest that I've already been driving two or three times this week. Also, that I'm quite happy to sit reading in the sun, and that will leave more room for the other Ladies. 'There is plenty of room. Afternoon tea is to be early, and we are all to be ready by half-past two.' At last, it is clear that between three and five o'clock this afternoon the house is to be empty of everyone but Mrs Baxter. So, on this glorious day we amble along the sea-front in a closed car without even the ghost of a sea-breeze.

Monday ₹ Matron is going to her electrician today and offers to take him my blanket to see if he can repair it. His verdict is that it would cost more to repair it than buy a new one, so back it comes. But for some reason I'll never know, because Helen has taken me shopping so often, and I need no one else, Matron brings me back two frocks, on approval, from 'her' boutique. It seems an odd thing for her to do. But both are well-chosen, and fit me well. If Helen thinks they suit me, I may keep one of them.

Thursday ₹ Helen is home after her fortnight away with Lucy. She looks rested. But she can't have had time to unpack before she speeds over to see me. We've had several record low night temperatures and she is shattered to hear about the collapse of my electric blanket and Matron's failure to repair or replace it.

'But she must have given you a hot water bag.'

'Darling, Matron does not have hot water bags here.'

'How could you let her get away with it?' And then, 'Look, there's somewhere I must go,' Helen says. 'No, don't come with me. I'll be back in half an hour.'

I might have guessed. In no time she is back again. Helen with loving kindness for me past belief, does something, where others just lament, and brings with her a new electric blanket.

'This woman is a sadist. You're not staying here. You're coming home to me. I'll ring the doctor and tell him, in the morning. Come home, darling, on Sunday.'

After Helen leaves, I find Matron, who is seldom visible, and tell her I'm going home on Sunday. She expresses regret. Twice she urges me to be sure not to tell the other Ladies, until the last minute, that I'm leaving here. 'They will be very upset,' she says coldly. But, she 'will be pleased to have me back at any time for a long or short stay. Perhaps if your sister needs a holiday ... ' Of course I'll tell dear old Mrs Dermott-Smith and Miss Laurie that I'm going. But certainly not either of the other Ladies. What puzzles me is how my G.P. ever came to recommend this rest home with its impervious Matron. He must have been pixilated by the facade tied up in its mean camouflage with neat bows of fake gentility.

Sunday Home. Like someone who has been blind, and at last can see again, I wander from room to room, touching old, loved familiar things. Then I go out to Helen and try my hand at trifling with household affairs. Together.

PRINCE EDWARD'S

March

Monday So it's back again to Prince Edward's. My favourite room too, with the trees and the Cathedral. And to the east there's a glimpse of rakish skyline to bring me back to reality. High-rises keep on outbidding birds and trees for more and more of the skyscape. But the Dandenongs, twenty or so miles away, this afternoon still drift in violet and azure cloud across the foot of my bed. Sister Mead is very much in charge, and the only Nurse Vlast is still on night duty, for good measure.

This time it is complete laziness for three or four days. And then, minor surgery and investigation. How often can one bend without breaking?

This is the end of my Indian summer, and there can never be another for all my wishful planning. Remembering this last spring and summer, unfolding week by week, is like watching one of those elusive French films, where time and place are still young, on an afternoon in summer, and everything a little understated. I see it now through a nostalgic golden mist where it is always afternoon. And faintly heard in the background there's a wayward little tune played on Pan pipes. There were highlights, too. That afternoon in November when Helen was involved with bridge, and I twisted the dial of my transistor to be told, without preamble, that history was in the very act of being made. Before the announcement ended, our Governor-General, Sir John Kerr, taking to himself more power than the

Queen herself, shot through the Constitution and dismissed the Whitlam Government while it still had a majority in the House of Representatives. As an airman of World War II, for Gough Whitlam there must have been a little irony in Sir John's choice of 11 November for this exploit.

Then there was another memorable day when instead of worrying Helen, or telephoning, I did my own shopping for Christmas – for the first time in years. My four great-nieces, when asked for suggestions, voted solidly for cosmetics. The two older ones knew exactly what they wanted. But nine-year-old Vanessa and her slightly older sister, who chose very glamorous talc, were, I think, inspired by the hidden persuasions of the family's new colour T.V. set. There are four chemists in our area, each housed far apart from the other. And each sold only one of the makes of these exotic aids to beauty that I'd set out to find. However, find them I did, after a very, very, long walk.

Then there was that minor heat wave when I was having such a tussle with an antibiotic, that even Helen's delicious fare seemed repulsive. Suddenly, Naomi came with a bowl of her own ice-cold gaspacho, with its little floating cubes of cucumber. Never before, or since, have I tasted anything as delicious as it was at that moment.

A good afternoon with Helen who insists, as she would, on coming again tomorrow. As I lie back watching the play of sun and shadow on the Cathedral grounds, I'm still storing away dateless remembrances of things past. And my day of days must be Christmas Eve.

Veronica invited Helen and me to dinner. Very generous of her, too, in the midst of all the various preparations for our kind of old-fashioned Christmas, especially as they were all setting out for the country at such an early hour next morning. Some time ago, the family promised Lucy to spend this Christmas Day at her home, instead of the usual celebration in town. Three hundred or so miles along the Hume Highway, all in one day, is, of course, beyond my scope. But a promise is a promise. So Nan, who was also unattached this day, came to share Christmas lunch with me – all perfectly arranged by Helen, beforehand. But this Christmas Eve: once more, Veronica and hers had made Christmas for me. And it was Christmas with all possible trimmings. The evening was cool. I'm glad I have a photographic memory because I can cherish that hour or two, forever. Here were we all sitting at the round, smoky glass dining-table, set with Swedish crystal. Two tall white candles burning with a little bowl of delightful small white flowers between them, and dishes of crystallized fruit to give colour. I'll forever see them all so wise, so gay, and so young.

This morning Gerard made one of his early morning calls. He seems to give a good many anaesthetics at the hospital and never forgets to have a word with me, often before breakfast. I've asked, especially, for him to give me my anaesthetic on Wednesday, not only because of his well-known skill, but because I've had several before, and I always have to fight my way out. I'd feel absolutely safe with Gerry. So when he tells me he can't possibly do it, I'm shattered. 'Don't worry,' he says, 'I'm getting you a very good man.'

Tuesday Gerry comes in very early to tell me everything is fixed. The anaesthetist is available, and will be in to see me later in the day. My surgeon to see

134

me, too.

Wednesday⚹ At a quarter to eight Gerard comes to see me again. It's always good to see him, but I've no worries. To the theatre at two p.m.

Thursday⚹ My first visitor today, as often happens, is Gerry, reassuring and always entertaining when he can spare the time. Then my friend and surgeon, to treat me like a human being and tell me more or less what he found yesterday. And also to say we'll hear from the pathologist in a few days.

My G.P. came too, to see what had become of me. And then Dr Tranter. I'm tired, but not too tired to thank him for being a wizard, not a doctor. His anaesthetic was sheer magic. I could never be afraid of one again, if he were in the offing. I'm more than lucky to have had all the skill and compassion that have come my way.

Midday, and time to watch for Helen. She comes – with a curving spray of those lovely little pink Singapore orchids that are a delight for an incredibly long time. Amanda, whose remembrance of me is evergreen, slips in for one moment with sad, too brilliant, Scott Fitzgerald's *The Great Gatsby*. Easy to read, easy to hold, too, in its lightweight, slightly theatrical Edwardian covers.

Saturday⚹ Regardless of his own week-end leisure, my surgeon comes to tell me he's just had word from the pathologist that I'm 'in the clear'. Helen will be happy. For me the waiting has been no strain. I may be a perennial rebel over small things. But these few years have taught me to quietly accept the immediate hazards. And as for the painful possibilities, they may never happen.

Sunday⚹ Kate and Sybil bring me a bunch of my favourite clove pinks from their garden and a divert-

ing choice of books. But best of all is their conversation which stays me better than all the flagons. Not
that brandy is to be despised. A whole week has gone
by with friends, flowers and books and the usual
superb care. All make you forget you are bed-bound.
They still give me treatment a couple of times a day,
and I'm not on my feet yet. But no problems, really.

Helen arrives this afternoon with a staggering bit
of news. Several years ago, when there were the first
signs that I might become a millstone, I telephoned
the best and most favourably known nursing home
round Melbourne, and asked if they had a single
room vacant. The Matron was sorry they had not.
And they already had a waiting list of five or six
hundred. From time to time I would ring this little
hospital to see if there might be a vacancy, but
without success. But my name was still on their
waiting list. A year or two went by, and there was a
new Matron. Yesterday, she telephoned my home to
say they had a vacancy with all facilities. Helen
quickly explained that I'd had some surgery at Prince
Edward's, and was unlikely to be up for a couple of
weeks. But she would speak to my G.P. and see how
much sooner he could give me a clearance. Unluckily, he was away for the week-end and could not be
contacted till Monday morning. Matron said she,
too, was going on week-end leave. Also, that she
could not possibly hold the room for me after
Monday morning. It was a problem, and Helen was
anxious and tense, as we talked round and round and
round it. At last, by slow motion, the easiest way
became clear. 'Darling, ring this Matron as soon as
she's available, and tell her I'll take the room. Then,
when you can at last speak to the Doctor, ask him the
earliest possible day I can leave here.'

Monday To have a room in two hospitals at the one time is reckless extravagance, and well beyond my means, but both Helen and I have tried so many possibilities of finding long term accommodation, where you can live even a little like an ordinary human being, that we think this chance is too promising to let slip.

Wednesday The doctor has been and says I can be on my way at the end of the week. It will be a bed-to-bed hassle. But this time, at least, I'm travelling hopefully. Sister Mead doesn't approve as they are still giving me treatment. She's a perfectionist, and, in her book, my rush to take off is premature. But at least, she says, she will hail me an ambulance. On more than one bleak day ambulance men have brought me to hospital with tender care beyond anyone's right or duty. But this time I can cope. Besides, if Sister had her way it would disturb Helen. For her, from old experience, ambulance spells drama. Veronica, whose car is much more roomy than Helen's, has already said she will drive us.

Two more days – and then? Call it 'Journey's End'. Of course that's not what my latest destination is really called. That name just spilt from my pen. It has an eerie sound.

JOURNEY'S END

Friday☞ Yesterday, Matron met us at the car. She wheeled me very quickly over the entrance where, on one side, windows run from floor to ceiling. At their feet, in window boxes, petunias blaze their trumpets of geranium-pink, violet, red and blue. Then I'm whisked down the long corridor to the second last room of the new wing. More white walls, with a high shelf surely eight feet long to hold flowers, prints, and any other bits and pieces I've brought with me. 'Facilities' are spotless and modern, and there are two big windows. One opens. There is also a door opening straight on to a path and a narrow strip of garden. A Japanese magnolia looks through the door. Its beautiful tracery of boughs and slender branches is so tall that it reaches for the sky well above the eaves. Matron is young and so swift she almost dazzles me. Not quite The Lady with the Lamp – more like a Ph. D. in public relations. Her vitality fascinates me. It flashes in a way that suddenly reminds me of the roadside oxyacetylene welders that I couldn't resist standing and watching when I was a very small child. But why is she here? An intensive care hospital, with its day after day excitement and challenges must be more fulfilling than watching life slowly ebb away, as it must, in places like this. It seems more than generous to use up this flood of vitality in the care of patients who are past healing. Others, less gifted, have the compassion and skill for this kind of care. At this point a delightful charge sister takes over. Helen and Veronica have made my passage very easy, but bed feels good.

Saturday Ghoulies and ghosties and things that go bump in the night have never worried me. But there was a slightly macabre touch about my first night here. It was well past nine. Since seven I had not seen one soul, nor heard a single word spoken. There was a bell, in case of need. But here was I, in yet another too-soft, strange bed. I'd brought two good firm pillows of my own with me. Even with them it would take more than these three flabby, oblong shapes already on the bed to bolster me up – breath being a ware I need. I was wondering what to do about it when the door opened. Her uniform was as dark as mourning. Without a word, she stood at the foot of the bed.

'Good evening, Nurse,' I said. She was middle-aged, with a tight chignon, and a kind of buttoned-up air. Her stony expression at once reminded me of hospital protocol.

'Perhaps I should have said, "Sister"?' I added, though she didn't seem to be in uniform.

'No.' She said. Her eyes were like shining black buttons.

'I'm Nurse Gummidge. I am a fully trained sister. But they don't recognize my certificate here. They call me a nursing-aide,' she said with a small, ironic smile.

'Did you know Mrs Battledore?' But before I answered, her expression had told me she didn't think I possibly could.

'It seems strange to see you,' Nurse continued, 'lying, tonight, in this very bed where she has slept for so many years.' There was no need to tell me she had made my bed with awe.

'Only a few days ago she was taken from us. The Dear Departed was a great lady.' I at once caught the idea of the importance of social standing. And also the impression that 'death' was a dirty word to Nurse Gummidge. 'And now she is gone from us – forever.' Not surprisingly the old dirge began running through my mind: 'This ae nights, this ae nights, Every nighte and alle, Fire and fleet and candle-lights ...'

'She always liked me to take care of her, poor Dear Departed soul,' Nurse Gummidge continued. Her glance wandered round the room. There was nothing remotely like a status symbol. There was no jewel case, no costly little aids to beauty. 'Well, we must all go.' A meaningful pause. 'When our time comes. Ring if you need anything,' said Nurse, and went on her way. Midnight. But I didn't set my fancies free. I read for another half hour. Then I fell asleep.

I never saw Nurse Gummidge again. I wonder if a legacy from the Dear Departed made her sudden retirement to the Sunshine Coast possible?

Friday Through the wide open garden door and window as a small breeze flickers, I can smell white jasmine. In full flower, it falls like a bride's veil over the tall dividing fence.

So many friends, books, flowers – it's weeks since I've unlocked my heart with a ballpoint pen. All these remembrances grow more and more precious. They can't be due to my charm or infinite variety. But parking here is easy. According to Helen it is a bed of roses, compared with the strategy and strife it takes to find a niche to park near hospitals on the edge of town.

Sandra, the nurse-assistant who sometimes puts my room in order comes from the Tyneside. She is big-hearted, loves music, and sings or talks non-stop. Although nine years away from home, her Tyneside accent is intact, and so is her very earthy vocabulary.

The old gardener is weeding the narrow bed just outside my door. That smell of freshly turned earth and new mown grass delights my senses and carries me away as the most exotic French perfume has never done.

Tuesday I'm sitting by the window reading. It's an afternoon of sun, and dancing, intertwining shadows of bough and leaf. Something draws my eyes away from the lines of print. I look up, and in the margin, at the top of the page, sits a praying mantis, green as an elm-flower. For a moment we quietly gaze at each other. Then she bows three times over folded, tiny feelers, looking exactly like a mediaeval abbess. She waits. I think the pretty thing is trying to tell me that someone has let her into my room, and will I please have the kindness to show her the way out. On the table beside me is a long envelope. Gently, so that she will not be afraid or hurt, I make a bridge of it from the page to the wire door. She passes along my bridge. Then I gently open the door to set her free. With dignity and grace she flies away into the garden. In all this coming and going there has not been one sound. But now the silence is like music... 'Pavane for a Praying Lady'...

It's well after seven o'clock and supper is running late. This suits me very well as I never have enjoyed going to bed with the fowls. At last, a pleasant nurse-assistant brings me my coffee. This is the only time she has ever seemed in the least perturbed. As she puts the tray on my table she says, with eyes flashing, 'Mrs X in Number 8 thinks she's at the Hilton.' Then we both laugh. Mrs X doesn't seem to bother too much to adjust herself to this way of living. Perhaps from lack of motivation towards better things, too many people in this little non-community settle down into committees of one. And so they become more and more ingrown.

Monday No visitors today. Almost the first solitary day since I've been here. Whatever I may miss in other ways, Helen, and the warm friends, who are still my friends through these drawn-out years, do so much for me to balance the losses. Today, I'm on my feet. Matron asks me if I will go with her and meet the others in the lounge. Some are too deaf to hear my greeting, and have no use for their hearing-aids. One or two reply, coldly but politely. On the whole they make me feel rather like Ruth among the alien corn.

One Lady has a glorious hair-do. Very dry, blonde hair dressed in a beehive, five or six inches high. The kind of thing the ladies of Marie-Antoinette's court favoured for great occasions. It must be a wig, and was probably a pretty considerable weight. This may be one reason why her face is so set and colourless. Perhaps, my last year's slacks and jacket are too inelegant for her. Hers are the latest cut. So are her smart, knee-high boots. She looks at me as if she couldn't care less.

Nearly all the ladies, I think, live in their own very small, private worlds. There is one exception. She is very old, but she smiled at me and waved cheerily as I gladly retreated, still on Matron's arm, down the corridor to my own room. Perhaps nursing homes would be more human if they were more even-handed. Here there are ten women to every one man. Is it that aging men are so much stronger they are not in need of professional care? Much more likely their span of life is shorter, so they die in their own homes, with dignity and in peace. Most men have worked for years at some trade or calling and have some skills and associations to look back on. Old men can be very entertaining to young children. On the whole, I suspect they are far more comfortable to live with than old women. Perhaps that is why they more readily find shelter with their own, and are less likely to be planted away by uncaring relatives in nursing homes. The longer I live the more firmly I believe with George Eliot that 'What we have been makes us what we are'. And that is especially true of the people I see here.

May

Thursday Today, Sister Gowan who takes such fine care of me, asked me if I would answer a few questions about life in hospital for a friend of hers who is doing a thesis for a higher degree in social studies. The interesting, easy question is 'Whether in hospital you feel cut-off from the outside world? If so, *why*?' Well, one never goes to theatre, concerts or art exhibitions. One can never browse through bookshops, and fascinating boutiques, for this and that. One never has a stroll in the hills, or the Botanic Gardens, or a day by the sea with sun on the water and a high wind blowing. I miss the heady scent of sassafras and the ice-cold breath of wild mint, and pennyroyal at that sharp bend on the road to Mt. Dandenong. But you miss more intimate things. Someone at hand to laugh with at the right moment. Someone to agree, or disagree with you. And someone to linger with you over those thousands of uninteresting, so-like-each-other meals. If you are a woman you may long for an intelligent man to talk to, even for a few minutes, to give you a different point of view. These days your busy G.P. hasn't five minutes to spare, even to talk about relevant things. Whatever he thinks, he confides to the sister who is with him as he walks out of your room. I miss other intimate things. An occasional dinner *à deux* at a well-set table, with candlelight, and red wine in a thin-stemmed goblet. And people round me. And paddocks starred with mushrooms that still glisten with dew as the sun rises. Especially, I miss children, and children's voices, at work or play. Even now, when I no longer travel hopefully, to enjoy happy, living things is a good prelude to journey's end.

Wednesday Not so many visitors this week. The days are cold and grey. There is a heat-bank which gives good warmth for one. But Helen, who hates the cold, still comes and spends the afternoons in her top-coat, wrapped in a rug.

Friday We have a new nursing-aide, Jenny. She's very young and slim and brown, like a wood nymph. Perhaps, I think of her this way because she talks to me about trees, and horses. In a way she is trapped, like I am. Her world is out of doors. This morning, after a very brief conversation about the new Leboyer birth method, and her own romance, she says, as she picks up my tray.

'You're gorgeous.'

'Jenny,' I reply, 'I'm not.' And then, I add, not quite so firmly, 'But you've made my day for me.'

She is not what they call a dedicated nurse. But, she's gay and compassionate, with a soft, clear voice. She took up nursing because to be a nursing-aide is only a one-year course, with the certainty of finding work, with good conditions, and a very fair wage at the end of it.

May, with all the good things coming my way, has been a long, dreary month. The garden door has often to be closed against wind and rain. This darkens the room and having to burn electric light for most of the day seems to bring back that old 'shut in' feeling I thought I'd shed forever. I have much more cause for being contented than many others have. But lately that moving 'Pas prisonnier mais...' speech in *L'Aiglon* haunts me.

A new nurse-assistant comes to make my bed this morning, Sophia, a well-rounded, smiling, fair-haired Greek. She has not lost her native accent, but how I wish I understood her language as she does mine. She says she comes from Athens. I tell her one of our English poets said Athens was a city 'violet crowned', and ask her is it true.

'Yes,' says Sophia. As she dusts my room I ask if they ever speak of Byron in Athens now.

'Yes,' she replies, looking very pleased. She is married.

'I work. My husband learns.'

'What is he studying, Sophia?'

'Everything,' says Sophia.

Friday I don't think Sophia is by any means an unlettered girl. But it gradually dawns on me that she is a diplomat who smiles and says 'yes' to everything – whether she understands you or not. And she mostly does not. But she is intelligent, and I would so much like to help her with her English. I've even enquired about a *Teach Yourself Greek* book to help me. But a hospital can't cope with this language problem. Especially as she says 'yes' so often in the wrong places. So pleasant, brave Sophia will soon be leaving us.

Saturday The winds have swept the last leaf

from the lovely golden poplar high up on the far side of the next-door garden. Its branches make a tracery of fine, black lace now, thrown over a cloudy sky. Bleak as it is this morning, the magnolia at my door is already covered in buds. But strangely, it is almost leafless. I've only just learned that with magnolias, unlike so many other trees, flowering time comes before, not after, the leaves.

Tuesday More and more of these hideous nights. They call him Tom. He's in a two-bed ward at the extreme end of the corridor from me. But no closed door can shut out that horrible ranting cry, that lasts for over half an hour, and ends like an animal roaring with pain. He is, of course, mentally ill. A young nurse tells me he is a paraplegic. This, I think, is in case I'm afraid he might be violent, as he certainly sounds. Sister Gowan, when I say he probably has plenty to rebel against, says he is not a paraplegic. He could be moving about. If he would. And he is not in bodily pain. It is not the voice of an old man. His lung power is terrific, and harrowing to listen to. No, she agrees, he's not an old man, about forty-five, and very big and powerful, so it is difficult to give him the necessary sedatives. The night staff is constantly changing. Only on two or three nights of the week is there anyone on duty who has the slightest control over him. Twice, since I came here he has been sent away for special treatment. This means two or three weeks' rest. It distresses me. His pain may not be physical, but his poor mind must be bedevilled. The deaf ones here are lucky.

I don't think all these attacks of chest pain I'm having lately, are entirely due to lack of sleep. I've already been given my various nightcaps, but though there is quiet, at last, I'm too disturbed to sleep, and much too tired to read now. This is one of the nights when I long for the peace of Prince Edward's. I long, too, for the comfort of Nurse Vlast, to plump up my pillows, with her smiling word or two that somehow can always put me in mind to sleep. Well, 'Joy cometh in the morning...' Perhaps.

June

Monday⟋ This June has dragged its slow length along. This morning at six the temperature was only 1°C. Much bed. Pain. And distress over things that I cannot alter, things that common sense tells me to accept, and simply not let myself be disturbed by.

It's a strange segregation. There are never less than three or four who are, mentally, very sick people. Their much heard voices are sometimes like shrill brawling, sometimes like off-key, sounding brass – to say nothing of the odd ones who, day or night, may wander pointlessly in and out of my room. They all need care and compassion. They may need it far more than I do. But, there should be a special place, and special skills to provide it for them.

The man who built these rooms planned them so that because of the positions of the two doors and the heat-bank there is no possible place for a bed, except in a corner, with the bedhead against one wall, and one side of it against the other. This wall has a built-in cupboard with shelves and space for hanging. The bed has to be moved out so that anything inside this cupboard can be reached. With the help of a nurse this problem can be solved. But, for anyone in the bed the door into the corridor is completely hidden, and so is anyone who comes through it to my bedside.

These intruders can be heard. They may open any closed door, but rarely, if ever, answer when I speak. The intruders who come occasionally when one is asleep, are probably harmless enough. But they would be less eerie, and easier to take if they were not invisible from both bed and chair.

Tuesday There seems to be a feeling of unrest right through the hospital. Another of Tom's more uncontrollable nights. He seems impatient of every-thing – at the very end of his tether. His cries grow louder and louder. More like a trapped animal than a human being. Tonight he sounds not so far from violence. Perhaps they will send him away for 'special treatment' soon.

Friday Half-past six on a winter's night. A golden disc of a moon rises in a deep black sky above the fence outside my window. A long-stemmed exquisite ghost of a rose lies across the moon. Almost every day since I came here last March, I've been able to see at least one lovely red rose climbing above the fence of that generous next-door garden.

Sunday Another of those nights. The hours of one, two and three are horrible, dreadsome little snails. I'm too tired to read. And I've had my full issue of aids to sleep. If only he would stop – and let me shake off this creeping pain.

Tuesday Temperature not much above freezing point this morning. But that's not the worst of chills. My morning paper says there are nearly ten thousand aged people waiting for beds in hospitals and nurs-ing homes in Victoria alone. Many have no insurance for private care. Mount Royal, the State's main geriatric centre, has a waiting list of over a thousand. In most cases this must mean incredible hardship for handicapped old men and women and their families.

But what is life for? What is the use of science prolonging life well beyond all previous expectation, if it cannot make life worth living?

A very brief visit from my niece Sally, and Don. She has just this morning been confirmed, so that they can marry next month in Don's old school chapel. I trust she will look nearer twenty on her wedding day than she looks today.

Thursday Elizabeth who now takes care of my room, and carries my trays back and forth, is a delightful human being. She has fine dark-violet eyes, set wide apart, and blue-black hair. She's not really large, but more a goddess than a nymph in build. I should think a professional photographer would welcome her as a model. Instead, she's a good wife and mother, works part-time here, and gives me the joy of looking at her as she dusts and admires some of my old bits and pieces. She is very interested in craftwork and has brought a long series of her fascinating craft books here for me to look at.

Elizabeth dearly loves a ball. Tonight, she slipped in to show me how she looked with her beautiful hair piled high, and wearing a long red dress. She seemed quite unconscious of her beauty.

Friday The heating system has broken down. Not quite the best weather for that. But they have given me, on request, a small but quite efficient radiator to take off a little of the chill.

'I've had such a happy afternoon,' Helen says gathering up her knitting.

'But darling, I do wish you wouldn't come here *three* times a week. Really. Once is plenty. You need some life of your own, outside these walls,' I tell her. But she's not to be persuaded. Matchless Helen. There is no one quite like her.

August

Friday⫶ This day week I woke as usual a little before five. It was still dark and the temperature was an icy 1°C. Today, a mere seven days later, the magnolia that spreads like a fan above the dividing fence outside my garden door, is covered in half-opened buds. It is hard to believe that after such intense cold two or three days of pale sunlight could so quickly promise spring.

And then Alice, friend of my youth, and my friend still, so generous, and with a most endearing sense of humour, without one word of warning, this afternoon wheeled into my room a colour television set. Though I've been so happy with Helen's portable black and white set, the very thought of seeing documentaries and plays and current events in live colour is sheer magic. At first I thought it was one of the family sets dear, big-hearted Alice was lending me while they are travelling. But it's new. And it's a most wonderful gift, not a loan, at all.

Friday⫶ Another tussle with angina that kept me awake till four this morning. I hate being sponged in bed, and wonder, brandy in hand, if with Sister's help a shower would be possible. It is after eleven. Without calling me cat, dog or devil, a nurse is standing at the foot of my bed and very abruptly says 'I'm going to make your bed.' She isn't. I'm too short of breath to move at the moment. She retires, taking her sense of compassion – if any – with her.

Saturday⫶ Just as it rose this morning, the sun shed a transient web of light over the magnolia at my open door. For a moment or two, each opening flower, carmine close to the stem, but with ivory petals, faintly flushed to scarcely perceptible elusive rose, swam in glory. At breakfast-time birds in the next door garden were singing a madrigal. Could any day begin better than this?

Monday Grace, my most infrequent, but most intellectual of all visitors has brought me some exquisite camellias from her trees.

Grace travels. Noumea, Israel, London, Belgium, The Hague. She sees them all with a painter's eye, and picks up impressions and ideas, like an elegant little bantam pecking grain.

Thursday T.V. has been really cosmopolitan this week. This is a night to remember. Shapira, an Israeli, conducted the Sydney Symphony orchestra in Beethoven's *Emperor Concerto*. An Englishman, John Ogdon, made that piano sing.

No visitors today. It's Sally's wedding day. Sally, Helen's first grandchild, and all of twenty years old, is marrying just as early as her mother Lucy did before her.

Yesterday, Helen came with a bottle of champagne for me to drink to their happiness. And a shade sadly, she reminded me that though Don and Sally pass close-by on their way from the church to the reception, they cannot call in to let me see her as a bride. It happens that someone on the other side of the family, who lives miles away and can't be at the wedding either, would take umbrage if she heard of it. Amanda, sensitive as ever to things that are dear to me, has sent a delightful bouquet of rose-pink hyacinths and boronia to console me for not being with them all on this day of days.

I watch the clock as the half hours tick by. On the air, as if to order, they are playing those lilting, sunlit dance tunes of Albéniz. Now Sally will be dressing. Los Angeles joins us with a group of de Falla's popular Spanish songs.

Later – It is well past five and the light is on. That lovely voice comes ringing and gay through this little room like wedding bells. Then the music stops. By this time Sally and Don will be wedded.

Though entirely without prejudice in all things concerning good wine, I hate to drink alone. So Matron, now off duty, comes by special invitation, to drink with me to the children's enduring happiness. It is almost dark as we take our last sip. It could be all the thoughts that have filled my mind this last hour or so, the music, and the good wine, too . . . the garden door is half open though the wire door is closed, but I'm certain I can see a shape, and something trailing like mist against the wire. A slight rustling. Then in walks Sally – a small Primavera, her dark brown eyes beaming with joy. But not only Sally. Don, the two bridesmaids, the best man and the groomsman all follow into the four-by-four space between bed and wall. A truly delightful invasion. Matron discreetly retires to make more standing room. But I haven't one sip of wine, or as much as a sweet to offer them. As the four attendants seem exceedingly light-hearted, this may not be missed. Don has been shorn for the occasion, and now looks as tall and handsome as he really is. All the lads startle me with very full-blown red carnations in their lapels, instead of the usual white ones. White carnations are right out, they tell me. I must be even more of a museum piece than I imagined.

This is Sally's day. Her straight-lined, white satin gown circles her slender neck, and long tight-fitting sleeves clasp the small wrists. On her shoulders a glowing cloud of hair the colour of wild honey rests smoothly as a page's in a Renaissance painting. And a simple wreath of small white flowers fresh from the garden keeps her short tulle veil in place. She still holds a very youthful bouquet of the same white flowers, starred here and there with what look to me like tiny golden daffodils. Primavera. This is how I will always see her, standing before me in this austere little room.

'Kiss her, Don.' This is the groomsman, name unknown, and a thought too sure of himself for the occasion. Don sat her beside him on the edge of my bed as if she were a child, put his arm around her waist and, to a laughing chorus, gave his Sally a schoolboy peck on her blush-rose cheek. I remembered days when my whole being sang 'My true love hath my heart, and I have his'. And I hoped that Don would know another way to kiss his bride. Five minutes more and they were gone, leaving me surprised by joy, if ever I was. Generous young Don and Sally to come this way and make a little of their happiness mine, as well.

September

Thursday No visitors today. This bed my centre.

Friday Mao Tse-tung died today, aged eighty-two, one of the few great men who have changed the world. My favourite of Mao's sayings is: 'Letting a hundred flowers blossom and a hundred schools of thought contend is the policy for promoting the progress of art and science.'

Saturday At tea-time another freak squall. Thundering rain, and hailstones as big as loquats battered and buffeted the magnolia. It swayed like a sailfish in a gale. After the storm a young nurse showed me one of those hailstones, yet a few buds still held. As the wind whipped its slender boughs against that solid fence I was afraid, with all the flailing, it must break in two. Yet now in the steady morning rain the lovely resilient thing is alive and waiting for sun to unfurl its last three buds.

Tuesday Dick came to see me today. A marvellous hour of talk. We glory in a host of radical ideas, and pool our enjoyment. It's a special kind of friendship, enduring because we both speak the same language. Dick brought me food for the flesh as well as the spirit – delicious grapefruit from his own garden, expertly prepared with a touch of finely chopped mint. His patients must miss him, for he retired early and is now involved, it seems, in the art of being a grandfather.

Monday The midday news says five hundred demonstrating black children have been arrested in Johannesburg today. When will *we* hear the cry of these children?

Wednesday The hot water system has failed again this week. The repairs on Monday were only temporary. The old story of having to go away and get 'another part' for replacement. This has taken four days and the water will not be heated until Sunday.

Friday There's a curious feeling of uncertainty and unrest all round us these past few weeks, and constant changes of staff. It must be bewildering to many of the patients to be handled so often by complete strangers.

More of these horribly disturbed nights. Most nurses don't know their patients, or their ways. This seems to make a good many patients increasingly insecure, and insecurity is one of the main problems, surely, of people who wander so disturbingly into my room at times. Yet, in many ways, it is very nearly an ideal situation compared with my previous sentences in nursing homes. This one is happy in its unusual matron, and yet, lately, she is less finely tuned to things. I'm convinced she has a problem, possibly more than one problem. And one we know little or nothing about.

Listened to an absorbing talk by Myra Roper about China. Who but the Chinese would think of naming a royal apartment 'The Hall of Earthly Tranquillity'? And how true would it be, in these nuclear, electronic days?

Saturday Outside for an hour this morning, after six long months inside the same four walls. They put me just outside my garden door in a swathe of sun. Just inside the door my transistor was playing Mozart's *Clarinet Concerto* – another kind of sun. The scent of leaves and grass clippings and of earth, and the tall white viburnum, heady like delicious wine, came in small wafts towards me. A bright ribbon of polyanthus was still flowering. A few yards away purple cinerarias were soaking in the sun as I was. There were white ones too, giving back a kind of sparkling shower. Then that unfamiliar, vast, blue roof of sky clouded over. A warning chill breeze drove me inside. But what a day – all this, and, in the afternoon Helen, too.

Sunday I've been re-reading Virginia Woolf's short stories – old favourites like 'A Haunted House' and 'The Mark on the Wall', and 'The Shooting Party'. What a way she had with words – but she knew people, and drew them in a timeless way.

Fragile, elusive Katherine Mansfield wears well, too. Of all the Bloomsbury group, Aldous Huxley was the bright star of the up-and-coming youth of my day. And yet, for all his wit and perception, reading him again, in the spotlight of experience, gives me a kind of feeling that he wasn't for all time, but simply for his own post-war age.

Tuesday In all these months my first night visitor. Emma turned eighteen at the weekend and today, lectures over for the term, she took herself off for her driving test. Borrowing the family car, her first drive was here to see me. At eighteen Emma now can record a vote. She can also marry without parental consent, though I don't think she ever will. Ours is an old friendship, not the average great-aunt and niece relationship. It began when Emma was about two years old and has continued with no thought of age gap and an enjoyable frankness on both sides. She was bubbling with life and the joys it brings. I can't believe one moment of youth is wasted on Emma. She left me stripped completely of the withering husk of years, forgetful of all that illness and time have stolen from me.

Wednesday Last night was strangely peaceful. Five hours' good sleep. Yet, today nothing is on time. Linen is in more than usual short supply, more strangers on the staff, and two very unruly patients close to my door. They sound as if they are not just ill. Part of the clamour could be unhappiness and insecurity.

Helen is away for a few days. Most of the people I know seem to be away – involved as mothers, aunts or grandmothers in these September holidays. You could close your door against the turmoil and watch T.V. Yes, indeed. But the Powers that arrange afternoon T.V. programmes take a shabby view of afternoon viewers' taste. They hoard the documentaries and good serials and plays for the evening.

Monday♫ From the lounge, five or six doors away, decibels galore of exotic sound. Mrs Hendel is giving one of her rare performances. It sounds like a slightly off-key, very scratched L.P. record – snatches of the mad scene from *Lucia,* followed by the waltz song from *Romeo and Juliet.* She has a fantastic range, and amazing volume.

Thursday♫ Seven a.m. on a calm spring morning. In the next door garden a dove is urgently calling 'I want you-ou-ou, I want you-ou-ou'. Again, and then again, in the distance. It sounds as if it comes through happy, faraway years that are all but forgotten.

Saturday♫ Matron is leaving. For several weeks she has not been quite with us – some involvement we know nothing about. She tells me she will stay here until a new matron is forthcoming. It will be hard to find someone to measure up to her. We shouldn't expect to harness her quality to this kind of hospital where the outcome of every case must always be the same. She needs the challenge of fighting to save lives. I think she would probably enjoy a refresher course in new nursing trends, too. For this enclosed collection of old ladies, and two or three men – it is in no way a community – her going will be a far bigger upheaval than any change of government in the world outside. Here nothing ever happens that is at all unexpected, unless it is traumatic. *Stop thinking about yourself.*

October

Saturday☞ Often, lately, I have that 'look-thy-last-on-all-things-lovely' kind of feeling. The solitude of a hospital room is different from solitude at home. This solitude of mine is only swept away by talk with the friends of my youth, or with the up-and-coming young who visit here more often than I dreamed they would. When they do come ideas bubble over because they have been corked up overlong.

Two or three times a week a very smooth, big jet-black cat parades along the narrow path still bordered with polyanthus, outside my garden door. I watch him anxiously. He looks at the birds with a nonchalant expression. Happily, he's too sleek and well-fed to bother about the chase. I've christened him Finnegan, after a friend with similar airs that used to belong to one of my neighbours.

Monday☞ Must look up 'works of supererogation'. I'm sure I've read somewhere that monks in olden days used to teach their flock that they could lay up treasure in heaven – in case of future need – by good works beyond the call of duty. This is what Amanda is always doing. Now she has brought me, before she has read one page of it herself: *Joyce Grenfell Requests the Pleasure*. It's one of the most bedworthy books that in all the years has come my way. She steps in the round from the printed page. On every page she makes you welcome, and often makes you think. Without one false step and with humour she conjures up her recollections of things past. It's a rare gift to turn what can be bitter-sweet into laughter, and be honest and generous at the same time. Thank you, Joyce Grenfell. And thank you, Amanda, too.

Tuesday Still more changes of staff – some due, they have told me, to bouncing wages cheques. This is outrageous, for patients' fees are high, and rising. In some way, Matron is deeply concerned. She is kind, but seems no longer interested. An agency sister who has never been here before, and one inexperienced nursing-aide had to cope with death last night. It was not unexpected. There were twenty-eight other patients, most of them problems, on their hands, as well. Both were strangers to us all.

Wednesday Bad nights and a conveyor belt procession of nurses. There must be a reason for this. It can't be coincidence. There seems to be a change in the type of patient, too. One, at the far end of the corridor, howls – there's no other word for it – at least three times a day. A strange, fractious, raucous cry, with amazing strength.

There's a wanderer who has come into my room disturbingly two or three times. Yesterday she strayed on to the tramline. 'Luckily,' they say, 'someone found her and brought her back.' Luckily? Does anyone ever wander away from happiness? These unhappy misfits must make life hard for the other women in the wards who can hear. In a room nearly opposite mine there is a patient who, night after night, shouts, as if she were being attacked. 'Police! Police! Get the Police. Murder, Murder.' She is mortally ill, but in no pain, whatever, Sister has told me. It seems as if these patients need expert psychiatric treatment and care of some kind. They take up nearly all of the present enduring nurses' time. Where does geriatric stop, and psychiatric begin?

So much of this makes me feel frayed at the edges.
Angina...

Saturday This afternoon there's to be a total
eclipse of the sun. The birds don't so far seem to be
disturbed. They were like a little orchestra of flutes at
about four o'clock this morning. Already the sky is a
blanket of dark cloud. I must switch on T.V. this
afternoon and try and see what happens. The birds
now sense something strange. They sing their evening song at midday, then vanish, today, as never
before. From Ballarat airport, T.V. gave a miracu-
lous cover of the eclipse. Even before half-past four,
although the day was mild, the air grew cold enough
in minutes to make me reach for my winter rug.
Gradually the moon completely covered the sun.
With one stride, darkness came. We could see the city
lights fully on. Then back at the airport, in seconds,
there was the mystical corona, giving enough light to
see the beauty of the smoky green, yet in some way
lucent, cloud that passed across the moon and let us
see the slowly emerging sun.

It must have been a moment of truth to an astrono-
mer or a physicist. It gave me back that elusive,
magical sense of wonder and belief that seldom lasts
beyond childhood. I wish Helen had been here to
share it with me. She is away in the country this
weekend with her family. Outside my door in a faint
glimmer of light, for one second, a bird sings. Then,
suddenly, it stops, as if it has made an embarrassing
mistake. A few moments more, and the screen showed
a strip of sea and sky that could have been a Condor
sunrise. Well before five o'clock it was broad
daylight. For that bare half hour I felt as if I knew
what it might be like to hold eternity in the palm of
my hand. It was exquisite, enchanted, and

unforgettable. A miracle to find oneself even a tiny, insignificant fragment of the glory of creation.

Sunday Not quite such a hectic night. I must make peace with myself. Keep remembering, even though you do live by proxy, there are meetings with friends, books and music to hold to your heart even here.

Monday Today my room is flowering. Bridal white azaleas, pink ones, too, and those little white orchids with cups flecked with violet, growing along slender stems, that they fly down from Singapore. There's a long-stemmed rose-pink carnation, too, ruffled like a peony. With wide-eyed pansies, and even an early sprig or two of lily of the valley.

Helen is here. The very trees outside my door are breathing spring. Happiness – if only for this afternoon. I can still enjoy things. Even in a long blind alley like this.

November

Monday Since March, there have been eight deaths under this roof – one a well-known woman journalist. Life for her had really ended some time ago. Such happenings are passed over in a very impersonal way, though never callously. Such is the pressure that each empty bed usually has a new occupant the same day.

Horrible shrieks and cries soon after breakfast. Is someone having a fit? Or, is she in desperate pain? 'Neither,' says Nurse, 'just Mrs Russell objecting to having her hair washed.' All this, from the far end of the hospital penetrates my tightly closed door. It must be shattering to be close at hand.

Just before breakfast Mrs Hutt walks in, for the third or fourth time this week. Most indignantly she asks, 'Why is Number 10 on this door today? The last time I came it was Number 5.' Tim, the cleaner, is quietly giving expert cosmetic treatment to my floor.

'No, it wasn't, Mrs Hutt,' he says. 'This has always been Number 10. Number 5 is up the other end.'

'It wasn't before today.' She's getting furious. '*This* is Number 5,' she insists.

'No, this has always been Number 10. Come on.' And very gently and persuasively, Tim at last manages to lead her away, in a manner far beyond the call of the pleasant man's duty.

Visitors sometimes speak of the sullen faces that line the walls of the lounge. I very rarely pass that way, but when I do, only one ever answers my greeting with a smile. The traumatic incidents never happen in visiting hours. The only explanation I can think of is that, in the interests of peace, tranquillizers are made to cast their spells over the afternoons. In the interests of sleep how I wish they could be more effective at night.

The exodus of nurses goes on. There are only three sisters left of those who were here when I came in March, and they are only here part-time. Some have left after four or five years on the staff. I can only think how selfless they must be to have worked so long in this kind of hospital. The more capable nursing-aides have gone, too. Perhaps it is being on the market for some months that makes 'Journey's End' seem so like a ship without a captain.

This has been a funny day. Tonight, at about half past nine Nurse was trying to persuade Mrs Hutt that it was time to get into bed, *not* to get dressed. 'Mrs Hutt? And why all this formality?' says Mrs Hutt.

Nurse: 'Because I've been taught to respect my elders.'

Mrs Hutt.' 'My name is *Florence*.'

Nurse: 'Very well, Florence, my name is Mary.'

Mrs Hutt then proceeds, quite happily to bed.

Wednesday 30°C. There is no ice. Helen comes from her air-conditioned home to sit with me in this hot little room. Today, result of blood tests. A potassium problem. There's a rumour that because of staff shortages all viable patients will be sent home for Christmas.

Thursday Yesterday, in face of strong, well-informed and organised protest, Canberra approved the export of uranium to all customers. Cash and carry. I feel cold inside, remembering how the Menzies Government, also against strong opposition, sold pig-iron to Japan. Helen and I remind each other of days when we saw the legend 'Pig-Iron-Bob' splashed in huge white painted letters on a bridge near our home. Stronger still is the remembrance of the way that pig-iron ricochetted to tear away our men's lives in New Guinea and Timor, and in the Pacific, too. And what about the radio-active waste? There's airy talk of safeguards. There's no system yet invented of absolutely flawless, fool-proof, waste disposal. And eminent scientists all round the world have said there is, so far, no safeguard against the lethal radio-active waste products from uranium.

Friday 30°C yesterday, too, and no ice again. Sister apologetically explains that the 'fridge' is only of medium domestic size, and in no way adequate for all our needs. This afternoon my Helen has brought me a plastic bag of ice-cubes from home. *Delicious*. I've an inbuilt objection to drinking lukewarm water, and that is all that is available here, these days.

Monday⌀ More in this morning's paper of the long lists of elderly men and women – almost 10,000 – waiting for beds in nursing homes. This must mean great hardship for some, but I wonder do they really want these beds? Of course, the severely handicapped need bed-rest with professional care. But, with the right kind of encouragement, there are some who could still remain individuals in their own home surroundings, in touch with friends and neighbours, and familiar things. There are many cases, where family team-work, instead of depending, as so often happens, on one overworked, devoted member of the family, and organizing help from visiting nurses and Meals-on-wheels could keep old men and women out of institutions, perhaps forever. They would, with few exceptions, be far happier. Condemn cruelty, racism, greed, if you like. But don't condemn old age to segregation.

Wednesday⌀ More new faces today, one to bring breakfast, another to make my bed. By mid-afternoon another relay will take over. Day by day, week after week, they come and go, like a travelling show on one-night stands. The only staff left that I know, of all who were here when I first came, are Matron, Sandra and Sister Pegeen. Sister is here only two nights a week, and hasn't any equal for dealing with distress. The rest I don't know at all. All are like paper cut-outs in uniform. Perhaps they might reveal some kind of depth if they were here long enough. As it is, they have less reality for me than the view from my window, or a passing train might have.

The doves are very vocal this morning. It sounds like a domestic crisis.

December

Friday⫇ Still out of action. Thrombosis. Already my radio has brought me Benjamin Britten's *Ceremony of Carols*. Perfectly trained children's voices add to their rare beauty, especially in this time and place. Suddenly, I remember how deeply moved I was the first time I heard these *Carols*. They were sung at dusk, by twelve schoolgirls as they slowly walked in, holding candles that lit their serious, shining faces. One or two voices had that lovely reedy tone that seems to desert even the very musical ones as they grow up.

The last few weeks we have had a full-time charge sister. Young, so not very experienced, but very well trained. She's pleasant, compassionate, quick-thinking and most dependable. It is good, after all the recent stopping and starting, to have someone like her around.

Saturday⫇ No supply of the special tablets I'm to take four times a day. One of the 'itinerant' sisters tells me they were ordered from the chemist two days ago, but they haven't come yet. Why the hospital deals with a chemist in a suburb several miles away from here when there is a well-established all-night chemist within two or three minutes' walk is a mystery.

Last night Sister Pegeen brought a packet of shortbread she made herself, as a gift for every patient. And she not only has night duty twice a week, she has a husband and growing-up boys and a girl at home to provide Christmas cheer for, as well.

This afternoon my missing tablets were found, in

the 'wrong' cupboard. I fancy there can be politics in hospitals, no less than in the world outside. This one is still on the market. Recent hopes of a sale have been dashed. They say because of the need for so much renovation, coupled with a very high price, and only basic equipment to go with it.

Monday In the last seven weeks the hospital chemist has billed me with enough sleeping tablets to last me for *five months*. I've protested about this to Matron who says she will see about it. I don't think I can do anything else, as this chemist is said to be a friend of the owner of Journey's End.

Thursday After a good deal of pursuit, and varied effort our young sister has arranged for carol singers to come here and sing to us tonight. She tells me none of the local churches could provide carols for our Christmas so she rang the Salvation Army. As so often happens they have saved the situation. And at this moment, we are enjoying the happy voices of the 'Salvos' carol singers, up and down the hall, and for a moment or two just outside my door.

Saturday Though off duty, our young sister came just after breakfast to bring me an exquisite, long-stemmed white carnation for her Christmas wish.

With superb stage-management by Helen, and strong support here, I did get from bed to darling Veronica's family Christmas tree and dinner. The house was a dream. I was not entirely without glamour, either. Modesty, perhaps, should censor this last remark.

Emma called for me in her father's car. 'I borrowed it, Auntie, because it's so much bigger and better than mine.' And off we went, with me feeling like a duchess escorted by Vanessa, who had come with

Emma especially to keep me company for the drive.

It was as good as an old-fashioned Christmas with the whole family can be. Three heavenly, happy hours. Then, deeply touched by all this loving and giving, it was back to bed for me.

Wednesday We really are 'with-it'. Today, one old lady was banished from the lounge until to-morrow for using very bad language.

Thursday My birthday, but well past the time when it's seemly to take note of it. Still, there was a stream of family and friends all day. Helen was prepared. She brought really iced champagne – in summer nothing is ever really cold here – an elegant cake, wine glasses, olives, nuts and all the other trimmings. Amanda came too, with a delicious heart-shaped cake of her own making. Almond flavoured, with icing to match, and garnished with a little white banksia rose. Amanda gives elegance to everything she touches. Today my cup runneth over. My glass, too, as Helen reminds me.

In the evening, while there was still daylight, dear, too generous Nils remembered the day and came, as he always does, with his birthday wishes, a sheaf of those lovely long-stemmed pink and crimson roses, and a huge box of liqueur chocolates. I wish I could give, give, give. Not because of all these delightful things given to me today, but for enduring friendship and long remembrance.

Friday From my pillows, two gardens away, I can see a magnificent golden poplar swaying above the roof. It is my weathercock. Buffeted by gales from north, south and west it sometimes makes me hold my breath for fear it should snap. But it stands up to the weather, and proudly lifts its golden head again, as if it were the spirit of all living things.

January

Saturday⟋ The Indian summer of a magnolia. This is the second time it has flowered since early spring. Today, there is just this single blossom to make me and the birds that are its steady visitors rejoice.

Several of the part-time staff have gone on leave to be with their school-age children. Three or four who have replaced them are younger and different – students. One is friendly, Cheryl. She has beautiful, very intelligent eyes in a fresh, moon face, and shapely hands that look as if she takes good care of them. Something makes me ask her what she does with her time when she is not carrying round trays and washing dishes. She replies with a soft, musical chuckle, that she is a fifth year Med. and is only working here at week-ends. She is doing a good, though not spectacular course. But she seems to me to possess some of the choice qualities that the world is looking for in its G.P.s. She has charm, too. On week-days Bridget takes her place. She's quick, dark-haired and lithe. She liked my Renoir print immediately. This leads to the revelation that she too, is a student, doing an honours course in Fine Arts.

Yesterday, the temperature was over ninety degrees, again, by the old reckoning. Hot food, and no ice. This morning, after last night's rain, the air is still cool and clear. But early as it is, the sun is already weaving a delicate shadow tracery of the magnolia on my wire door. According to the weather bureau we're to be grilled and steamed again today.

Mrs Russell, completely at sea, wandered in and

out of my room three or four times last night. Her eyes gave me an uneasy feeling. She seemed to be prowling. It's disturbing. But it would take a nurse apiece to keep these poor disorientated beings from making life uneasy for the rest of us.

Wednesday Three degrees warmer than yesterday. You could fire pottery in this little furnace of a room today.

Bridget comes to take my breakfast tray with a massive volume of Post-impressionists, from her father's library, she says, to *lend* me. I'm always deeply touched when the young make this kind of gesture. The reproductions, all in colour, are richly exciting. Especially to someone who hasn't seen an art exhibition in years. It's a splendid book. And so generous of Bridget. How she managed to even carry it from her car I don't know. It has a very solid linen binding, apart from all the prints, and is heavy for me to move an inch. But I can, and will turn its pages – and will, over and over.

Sunday Out of action these last ten days.

My little pot of lily of the valley has died down to the last leaf. I've asked Mr McLeod, my friend the gardener, if he will plant its bulbs in the strip of garden just outside my door. He solemnly warned me that they may never come up. And even if they do, they can 'wander all over'. I told him that would be good.

Monday This morning, Mr McLeod sent me, by Nurse, a big, highly 'technicolour' card of lily of the valley – people sometimes astound me with their thoughtfulness.

Tuesday This afternoon the owner came to take elaborate measurements, at last – for repairs that he will not carry out. He's a trendy, very presentable, professional man. Surprisingly young to be the owner – freehold and all – of a property like this. They say he owns a farm and other properties as well. In manner, he's smooth as glass, though not so transparent, yet with a certain charm. Not unlike David Niven, when he plays smooth young men on the Riviera, or in the West End. Wealth is not enough for this owner. He lets his greed grow fat on the deprivation of frail, handicapped men and women who have not the will nor the wit to stand up to him. For over six months, immediately outside my window, whenever it rains, you can hear water pouring down, like a hydrant from the broken pipe. At night, it is torture, and most hostile to sleep. He will do nothing about it. Today there's a still, green pool, just outside my door. When I first came here the damp patch on the ceiling was like a mushroom. Now it is the size and shape of a cucumber. I don't envy Matron, yet she seems to cope with most of these passing problems. Probably she's living in expectation that a better time will be had by all if, and when, we have a new owner.

Wednesday Late this afternoon the lady with that intriguing, ash-blonde, beehive hairdo, came, unheralded, into my room. She had dressed for the occasion. With a pretty, meaningless smile she wished me a happy New Year, and then bowed almost to the ground. Her long pale blue evening gown set off the remains of what must have once been pink and white prettiness. After her bow, with perfect timing, she vanished, without another word. I think she has a story. Perhaps she was once in show business. This was indeed, a performance. In some remote way she seemed to enjoy it. So did I. Sister says she is well over eighty, that the incredible hair is all her own, and she hasn't a sign of a wrinkle. She has a will of her own, and is often away with the fairies. But to me she was charming, in her fantastic way.

Friday☞ Another of those 38°C days. No ice. No air-conditioning.

Wednesday☞ Geriatric is a cold, uncreative word. It has no heart. It's fatalistic. And it reeks of mortality. I've learnt that it is possible to have medical training, and still not be able to grasp that people old in years are not necessarily senile. Here, this syndrome is taking over – atrophy, apathy, endless, meaningless babble – mental collapse. It's a Pandora's box that holds nothing but distress. Nobody has thought to add any kind of hope. Why?

I'm sure some kind of activity would help most of these insecure, unhappy people round me. In all three nursing homes of my close acquaintance there hasn't been a sign of equipment, and no place where it could be used, for occupational therapy. Happiness has come to older men and women, as well as the young, in sheltered workshops. You are an individual when you are working at a craft, however simple. You may talk to your therapist, or to someone working beside you. Conversation is a deep, human need. Words can create thought, as well as conceal it. Meaningful speech is one of the essential human freedoms that can be encouraged and cherished even in nursing homes.

Thursday☞ Early this morning, while the change over from night to day staff is taking place, unimaginable decibels, until half past eight, at intervals of less than *one second*. With heavy demands of helpless and incontinent patients to be met, and because the hospital has been under-staffed since before Christmas, it is some time before anything is done to calm him down. Overworked nurses are not to blame. But for anyone with average hearing, over an hour of this clamour that no door can shut out, is almost unendurable.

Tom is more than six feet tall, with girth to match. He's another car-crash victim and thinks that he is paraplegic. He can use his hands to some effect, and like some of the others here, he might be made happier with some simple form of occupational therapy. Twice since I came here Tom has been sent away for shock treatment. He fights with uncommon strength against the sedation he so desperately needs. After a good hour and a half those cries of 'Nurse, Nurse, Nurse' become less frequent. Then, at last, they fade out...

That bird is beating beating against my ribs again ... trapped in my chest, so often these days.

Sunday Bells. Bells. Bells. Oh, noisy bells be dumb. At two o'clock this morning the lady across the hall began ringing her bell and calling for Nurse. She quickly received attention – with loud, overbearing complaints. Within minutes her bell was ringing again, and Sister who was in a ward at the far end hurried back. The ringing of that bell and those incessant high-pitched demands go on and on. They say she has no pain.

Wrenched from sleep by more bells and loud cries of 'Murder – murder. Get the police!' I switch on my bedside lamp. It is half past two. I am now very wide awake. Could she possibly have been attacked? Seeing my light on, Nurse hurriedly assures me she is not in pain. And no one has attacked her. I doze, but only for a few minutes. Again she wakes me. After another wide-awake hour, I reach for my book. Strange that it should be *War and Peace.* I read till six.

Already the sun was spreading a bright patina of gold over the poplar a few doors away. Then I fell asleep.

Just before seven Sister comes with needle poised for action on my thigh, which is beginning to feel like a pincushion. Then breakfast and another day.

A psychedelic collection of sedatives, not taken until around eleven o'clock, should give me a fair night's sleep. Today, because they haven't been allowed to do their work I have a wretched hangover.

Very late this afternoon, Rose dashes in with a heaven-sent baby bottle of champagne.

Friday 4 a.m. Wakened by sounds of a terrific struggle opposite my door. Can it be death? A fit? The two very good nurses on duty tonight answer my bell. After investigation both decide it was nothing worse than nightmare. Which sounds quite distressing enough for the victim. Awake for a couple of hours – but tired past reading this time.

Helen's birthday and very good she is to look at in her white and navy silk. As she passes by the lounge on her way in, an unknown Old Party calls her over: 'You shouldn't wear that. It makes you look washed out. Wear pale colours.' Still chuckling, we sip something ice-cold Helen has brought for the occasion. Go not, happy day.

Saturday Angina ... Another itinerant night sister who couldn't care less.

Sunday Finished Patrick White's *A Fringe of Leaves*. It may not be a great novel. But only a great writer could tell Eliza Fraser's story and capture and hold belief in the strictly unbelievable, quite as Patrick White has done. And I can't think of anyone else writing today with that same deceptive simplicity, invention and creative integrity.

After nearly five months my deep purple African violet is still gaily flowering, obviously rejoicing in this month's long heat and humidity.

The white jasmine still rambles its snow-white way over the fence outside my windows. Today, at last, it is cool enough to keep my door on to the corridor closed to the spasmodic human noises and three different T.V. sets, on either side, and opposite me sounding three different programmes, at greater volume than you would think possible. Closing the door narrows my world in one sense. But at least it lets me hear my own transistor. As the days and hours and weeks crawl by, music is more than ever escape and healing in one.

March

Tuesday ⫶ Ten minutes walk in coy, uncertain sunshine with nice Sister Mac., lately here from Derry. She has a delightful accent – not quite Lowland Scots, and not Dublin. It's something between, and has its own music. Very good to be out of doors, at last, with a furtive, small breeze in my hair, after these weeks of lying on a fracture board. Which seems to prove a disc can be no use whatever, except when it is in its right, true place. Curiously enough it was my heart specialist, not my G.P. who discovered this disc of mine had, most improbably, slipped. Sister Mac., like so many of her more pleasant forerunners, after less than a month here, leaves us the day after tomorrow.

Friday ⫶ No hot water for the past three days. Lately, Matron has been on short leave several times. This time they say she has a virus. I suspect she has her own problems, and no doubt feels the stress of things here, as others, from private wards to kitchen feel it, as well. Helen at Mount Martha for a long week-end. The weather has suddenly turned cold, and she so loves the sun.

Thursday Exactly one year today since I arrived here. My next door neighbour has been here more than four and a half years. I do not think of living so long.

No visitors. To amuse myself, with the aid of an old atlas and scanty shipping advertisements in this morning's paper I plan cruises to far countries I will never see. First, that slow boat lingering round the isles of Greece. Then to Italy in search of the Renaissance. In the spring I'd go to Warwickshire and Shakespeare's England – Stratford to see Ann Hathaway's garden. Was Shakespeare remembering it when he put all those lovely cottage flowers into *A Winter's Tale*? I might even find that bank where wild thyme blows, and primroses and nodding violets too. But before England, on to Vienna to catch just one performance of *Rosenkavalier*. Stop. This infernal, roving spirit inhabits a more and more useless body. But it can be fun.

Tuesday New therapy. My G.P. says I must get away from here sometimes. Home to lunch with Helen is his suggestion, maybe once a week.

Things are insecure and far from happy, still. There must be a climax before long. A flurry of spring-cleaning that has filled the past ten days or so could be the prelude to a rumoured take-over. Late this afternoon another inspection by three or four men who look like doctors. Winds of change?

Sunday No church service this morning from the lounge T.V. Have the ladies no longer religion?

Generally, with my door tightly closed no straining of ears is needed to follow it. They say one or two of the 'congregation' listen. This may be a matter of routine. It is easier for busy staff to keep an eye on their charges when they are gathered together. Loneliness is part of their unrest, as well as the insecurity that comes from almost daily changing staff. It could be a good life, within limits. There is plenty of scope for it. But it would take a trumpet call of sounding brass to put life into the still sad music of humanity at Journey's End, these days.

Tuesday ꝏ Helen agreed with me today, that for the past few months there has been nothing here like the compassion, or the professional nursing skill of shabby, old, underprivileged Haddon. In this crisis, whatever it may be, the whole atmosphere has changed. My two acquaintances in the rooms on either side of mine feel this, too. We ask no questions. If you live in a nursing home it's a good idea to keep clear of its politics.

Wednesday ꝏ Every day I'm walking from my room once up the corridor as far as the lounge and back. One or two of the women, sitting regimented in their chairs along both walls begin to recognize me, and sometimes speak. There's never a book or a daily newspaper among them. No knitting needles, no little tables with cards set out for a quiet game of patience, or dominoes, or even for a jigsaw puzzle. Just where does mute, dull acceptance end, and apathy set in? Not one syllable seems to pass between them. Work that is easy, experience of the small everyday things, of loving and giving, with just a little help could do something to turn this minus living into a small human plus. Can't someone convince the people who have power over life and death in places like this that simply to use what faculties you have can be a kind of happiness?

Sunday Out to a delicious lunch at home with Helen. In a gracious room with a perfectly set table: A delight. But home for a few hours is too bitter-sweet to happen often. The day must always end here.

Back in my room at five o'clock my evening 'meal' arrives, even before my coat is off. The meal consists of four little triangles of tomato sandwich, without salt or pepper, and a pot of black coffee. The next meal is breakfast at 7.30 – orange juice, if any, coffee and two rounds of toast, provided there is no bread shortage. If there is, it's a slice and a half.

Still new faces. With two or three pleasant exceptions it is hard to believe most of these nursing-aides are trained. They are kind enough in their own rough-and-ready fashion. Often when you thank them their brusque reply is that they are paid for it.

Two magpies are carolling in a tree in the garden next door. A sound I haven't heard for a year. Compensation for some of the things that beset us here.

Tuesday This morning my own spot of drama. A hurried injection – pills – brandy – pills etc. Luckily Matron was back on duty. She and the young nursing-aide with her gave me expert care, and were so good to me – even in very small things. I was not interested in lunch. But someone brought me chicken. It was dark and very mature. It looked as though it had come from a natural history museum. And that is exactly how it tasted. Not that it mattered. I only took one small bite. I wasn't hungry.

Thursday Very early this morning blue-eyed Sigrid, aged three, calls to see me. She stands by the bed, her shapely head in its fine silky thatch, close to my hand. With a little prompting, on both sides, we tell each other the story of the Three Bears. Already a lovely mind lights her small face with innocence and wonder that are infinitely touching.

Since Christmas we have had a new charge sister. With a coarse loud voice and heavy foot, she has the classic qualities of a sergeant-major. In the early morning she trumpets like an elephant for her first hour or two on duty. This month I've had my first experience of a male 'sister' and a male nursing-aide. At the end of the month my impression is that, by and large, both are good. Peter, the 'sister,' is very perceptive, better trained and more intelligent, compassionate and professional than most of his opposite numbers, who have been here lately. Helen, with one of her quick flashes of insight, says they need to be just that to overcome the prejudice that still exists against male nurses, in general. Unluckily, Peter is only here for two or three sessions a week.

Today the owner requests payment of fees four weeks in advance. He has no sense of humour. And not many of the other hallmarks of humanity, either. A terminal patient would have to be verging on delirium to agree to this. Any of the rest of us could die well within his four weeks. In these days of inflation, and falling incomes that once were fixed, and which most elderly people live on, to many patients this demand must be very disturbing. Coming from a wealthy professional man and a shrewd investor, there are one or two harsher words than 'disturbing' to describe it. Meantime, I shall treat it with 'ignore', to quote one of my younger nieces.

Today Helen and I indulge in a little not so innocent merriment at the owner's expense. Florence Nightingale's warning that 'The first requisite of a hospital must be that it does not do the patient any harm', is not in his book.

April

Friday Helen brings me peaches, green and purple grapes, and figs, as good to look at as they are to taste.

Tuesday Sister brought me four tablets instead of the usual three this morning. I had to get a nurse to find her, and ask her which one I should *not* take. It may be that all four were intended for some other patient. She has made this mistake three or four times – with no apology or regret. Sister's trouble is that she knows everything. But everything. These mistakes of hers have crystallized into resentment towards me. I wonder what the result is if such mistaken doses are given to patients who don't know whether they are Arthur or Martha. Could swallowing the wrong pills have anything to do with part of this trauma we live through week by week?

Amazingly hot for April. 31°C again today.

Thursday The temperature has dropped sixteen degrees since Tuesday. Helen finds the cold here very hard to take. The hot water system has broken down, too. This is the third time in less than a year. The last breakdown was only six weeks ago and lasted about five days. There's an emergency service to deal with such breakdowns. But this seems to be something we have to put up with, like the shabby, repulsively stained bed linen, and general disrepair. Yet fees rise every few months. It almost seems as if these three failures of the hot water supply, each one lasting several days, might be used by our owner as a means of saving gas and electricity.

Helen brought me a sheaf of daffodils this afternoon. In this grey weather they make me think of the sun lighting up Sigrid's golden head.

Saturday For several weeks all through the night, every single hour, I've switched on my lamp to see what time it is.

Easter Day Happy Easter. Hot water at last. And a tiny Easter egg from darling Vanessa, tied with red ribbon to a knot of dried wildflowers. Vanessa already knows how to spread the joy that came into the world with her. To Helen's today for lunch and happiness.

Angina. Peter is on duty. He has a wonderful way with pain.

Tuesday Last night another witches' sabbath. In a ward two doors away a patient who has only been here a week became unmanageable. Luckily, her room-mate had gone home for the Easter holidays. There was trouble in the wards at the far end, as well. Nearby, this unhappy soul was hearing voices and believed she was being pursued by some evil force – man, beast or devil. Who knows which? She raced down the hall, with terrified cries of 'Don't let him catch me. Don't let him catch me.' She fell, near my door, badly enough hurt to need stitches. Neither nurse could calm her, hard as they tried.

Suddenly I remembered. Her voice was not harsh, like the others. She spoke with an accent like somebody I once knew. Liesel. The gentle charming Viennese doctor – one of the intellectuals the Nazis forced to scrub filthy pavements, and worse. Eventually she escaped to Melbourne with her child. She made a good life in her own field. But Liesel did not live to be very old. I never knew what happened to her husband.

Something makes me wonder if this tragic night is one more echo from a concentration camp.

At three o'clock a doctor arrived. He is a G.P. locum, not the specialist she needed. But he managed to sedate her at last. Towards morning I slept, too.

There are now five mentally ill people here – without the 'odd' ones – and no special means of caring for them. A night sister who has had experience of these cases says private psychiatric hospitals will not keep them, once they are past the more acute stage, if they are over sixty. Because they live too long. So once more, the small geriatric nursing home gives shelter and care to the dispossessed and the rejected. Surely there could be a community hospital adequately staffed and managed to cope with this kind of lingering, terminal illness. Sister also tells me a specialist can order tablets to banish those voices.

Pitying this sad, demented human being doesn't help her, and it shatters me. I have no fear, only horror and deep distress. Yet, I hope she doesn't visit me at night, as two of the others already have done. This is something more tragic than the disorientation, irresponsibility and loss of memory all round me... More angina in the early hours.

Wednesday This morning Matron called in a psychiatrist. Sometimes I feel I'm living in the kind of grotesque hospital that Hogarth might have painted. Other times it's like a horrific *avant-garde* play without solution or sublimation.

Friday Helen has come to see me five times this week. Chest pain pretty often lately. I wish I could have two or three hours of unbroken sleep. In this haunted, traumatic world it seems odd that to try to keep sane I cling to this scruffy little much scribbled-over and interleaved diary.

More of those loud confused cries over the way: 'Police. Get the police! I'm not mad. Give me a drink.' Then follows argument over and over it all with nurse. He's very patient and quietens her at last.

Too tired to write. Wide awake, but too tired to read tonight. These terrible, less than human sounds bore like blunt instruments into your senses. And yet, perversely, they sharpen your awareness almost past bearing.

Saturday Tonight Artur Rubinstein, aged ninety, in a B.B.C. radio interview from his elegant flat in Paris, with his Chagalls and Picassos round him, his wit, his panache, and a voice, clear and musical, as well. At ninety. The talk was illustrated with his own records of Chopin's *Nocturnes*. I heard him play them when he was in Melbourne over ten years ago. His intense delight in an artist's use of words came through. He insisted he didn't 'love music'. 'I *am* music,' he said, adding that he thought he was the luckiest man he had ever met. I don't remember ever hearing talk as original, and witty, with that amazing savour of youth and experience. He doesn't believe in the ideas people father on God. But he says he loves, respects, and is grateful to the Power within him that is part of some Power at the heart of the Universe.

His humour is dry. He says Ravel was very good to him, but he was good to Ravel, too, because he didn't say in his book how Ravel, himself, played. Throughout the interview he sounded not a day over fifty.

Sunday Sandra, from the Tyneside, now addresses me as 'Duchess' – possibly because I'm not given to four-letter words. Young Nurse Janet calls me 'the chirpiest patient in the hospital'. Eirene would like to know if I was once an opera singer? Very flattering – but not a bull's-eye among them.

More angina. Peter was on duty. More than most nurses he seems to know how to make the pain more bearable.

Tuesday⫰ The two worst psychiatric patients have gone. The staff, always with compassion and courage – with the exception of the sergeant-major – have fought a desperate, losing battle, and only one had any training or experience with such cases.

A little peace has slid into the place. An almost audible peace. And some sleep, too. The disoriented, insecure people who always stage their own scenes in these nights of crisis have calmed down. It almost seems as if they have been using their own wanderings and rantings to secure attention. For even here, life is competitive.

Saturday⫰ I've just read that at sixty-one Leonardo da Vinci injured his right hand, and then taught himself to paint left-handed. It was after this that he painted the Mona Lisa. Nothing geriatric about that.

The isolation of elderly people is convention in a very ugly form. But what chance has anyone of changing man's inhumanity to man when Tasmania, just across the water, is restoring the tragic penal settlement at Port Arthur as a *tourist attraction?*

Sunday⫰ With Peter's help, out to Helen's for lunch. Much delight at being home. Then back here. Still, if there were no shadows, I must believe, there would not be such wonder in light.

Another sketchy sleep. Up in the wards their cries are like retarded children's, but their voices are even more penetrating. Nearby the recurrent cry, 'Nurse, Nurse – Sister, Sister – I'm in agony.' That voice, desperately strong, then loud groaning comes through my closed door with T.V. running. At last silence. Her poor mind must be wandering. They say this illness is affecting her brain, but she's not psychiatric like others are.

Wednesday Matron is back. Buoyant, with all her former interest and enthusiasm ... The hospital is recovering, too. Even the charge sister is well toned down when Matron is here. It's less depressing – more friendly sounds of life, and of things moving, perhaps towards this change of ownership. Fervently I wish it could be.

Monday For two hours tonight more screams of 'Sister – Sister – I'm in agony.' It must take uncanny strength to keep up that sound. At last it dies away. She must be exhausted. So am I.

Wednesday After another night of alarms and excursions, this morning, Matron sits in my room and wisely and gently talks to me. She's not insensitive to the bruising and breaking I'm taking as a person. A couple of hours or so, even every day, with Helen, or with friends, can't cancel out the trauma of all these endless waking hours. The schizophrenic Viennese lady is away for intensive treatment. Her room will be kept for her. Because of her age the psychiatric hospital will not keep her, once she is past the acute stage. Then this geriatric nursing home takes over.

Sunday With Helen to Amanda and Edward's to lunch. My G.P. insists on this new therapy. Delightful while there. But not for the two days that come after. A bit like the story of the actor who gives the performance of his life, then goes from the stage to his dressing-room – and dies.

Tuesday Last night at about twelve someone

suddenly switched on my big overhead light. I asked 'Who is there?' No answer. Then again, but still no answer. I rang. Twice. Nurse came hurrying down the corridor. The light had already gone out. The L-shape of the room makes it impossible to see who comes in the door. I wasn't afraid. But I was deeply disturbed. Perhaps because of the eerie silence. I hadn't heard even a footfall. Another of those sleeping-waking nights that leave me too limp and tired for another day.

Wednesday Last night the patient who was opposite me died. Eight have gone on their way this year. All seemed to have been loved and well-remembered. This time there's no word of remembrance or regret. She seemed friendless. The only tenderness I've heard is the quiet weeping of the schizophrenic who shared her room. Perhaps distress made her switch on my light, so eerily, in search of comfort last night.

Thursday Matron becomes more and more professional. Her fine perception makes her good with all kinds of people. She can always calm the deeply disturbed ones, and often communicate with them when others fail completely.

Friday The hospital crisis is moving towards a close. An end is in sight to inadequate and constantly changing staff, shortages in the kitchen, and revolting bed linen. Today, we have been told there is a complete change of ownership. A medical association in a comparatively new field takes over.

Today, thirty towels have been found planted in someone's locker. Also a tea-pot, an alien stocking, and a hat. None of much account. The snapper-up of considered, as well as unconsidered trifles, is known, and loved, by nearly everyone. Rather an eventful day. At six tonight there was a freak storm. As far as I could see from my windows there was unbroken lightning. No flashes. Just a wall of steady, pink flame. Then torrents of rain and hailstones much bigger than mothballs. Constant blue flashes were coming from a little white car parked near the entrance Nurse told me. I really thought the storm must have struck an oil rig in the bay and that we were getting reflections from the fire.

Sunday Waited all day for Mozart's *Oboe Concerto in G*. Sheer ecstasy. Brought my own kind of cup and saucer from home. I absolutely refuse to drink from any more cracked tea cups.

Wednesday The garden runs wild. No one has touched it for six weeks. Long sprays of jasmine are twining themselves through the magnolia. I hope they won't hurt the swelling buds. Last week's storm took a good many. There will be fewer flowers than last year.

Much less bedlam the last few nights. Sleep for two or three hours without a break, which is heaven.

Thursday Watched another day come in. Long, grey clouds. A glimpse of wan sky and against it, a little to the south, a tracery of fine black boughs and branches. Very like a Japanese print. It is the golden poplar, leafless, but beautiful even in this grey half-light.

Saturday The tablets prescribed for me four times a day are missing again, this morning. Our charge sister has been on duty since Monday so she must have known the supply was running out. I need one. Now. But I can't protest about it this time. Last time I did. Very mildly. But she's a bully, and I can't take her bullying again. She seems to think I'm here for a holiday. Probably because I'm continent, occasionally ambulant, and never, except under stress, a bell-ringer.

Matron is taking day and night duty, at unexpected times, with staggering results. Late this afternoon my tablets were found in the 'wrong' cupboard by a sister who only comes for one session a week.

Tuesday ✐ Hear Mrs O'Hara, a sprightly, slim eighty- to ninety-year-old, scurrying past my door, like the White Rabbit.

Nurse: 'Where are you going, Mrs O'Hara?'

Mrs O'Hara: 'Hunting.'

Nurse: 'What are you hunting?'

Mrs O'Hara: 'I can't tell you.'

Nurse: 'Why?'

Mrs O'Hara: 'Because it is too rude.' And she pitter-patters away, with a laugh like little silver bells.

Sometimes she comes into my room in the early morning, in nothing but a pretty nightgown, to ask me the time, or to ring for Nurse for her.

Wednesday ✐ Today our new owners have taken over. An ample supply of spotless bed linen and bath towels is an immediate celebration. The entire staff is on three months' probation. There will be rehabilitation here, and the purely geriatric will be gradually phased out. Matron, most happily for all, stays with us.

Tuesday ✐ Sunrise at 7.20. Pink clouds, like flamingoes flying through light mist. To be remembered as a joy forever.

Wednesday ✐ The Queen's Jubilee address is on the air ... A suddent thrust of pain close to each armpit. In my jaw. Flowing down my arm to my finger-tips. *Please. Please.* It's in my throat too. I ring my bell. It was nearly an hour before it was answered, by the charge sister. Standing at the door she asked what I wanted. I gasped, 'An injection please, for a very severe chest pain.' Still at the door, she barked, 'You're a selfish, inconsiderate woman, Miss Newton, ringing your bell and bringing me away from my patients.' She was loud enough to be heard right through the hospital – and the kitchen and carport, as well. With what little breath I had left I said ... 'I hope you have an attack of angina before the year is over, Sister.'

With all my heart, I wish now I hadn't said it. I've never in my life cursed man, woman or beast, before. She went without a word, and sent an inexperienced nursing-aide of twenty to give me the morphine injection. Probably she was much gentler than Sister would have been. Matron was not here today.

Friday Two exquisite camellias from Lorna. A kind I haven't seen before, so soft and fine you almost feel they will take flight on their pale-rose petals ... Lack of compassion added to more of these hideous nights is shattering my will to accept what is and must be.

Monday Helen to see me and Rose, too, with the first violets of the year. They have a heavenly scent of spring in all this cold.

Thursday June is over. Very cold. My paper says it's the rainiest June for over a hundred years. No wonder it's the closed season for visiting. But David comes every two or three weeks. And always, Helen.

July

Friday Wakened at half-past three with blaring T.V. or transistor. They are very busy at the far end, but eventually someone turns it off.

I'm beginning to be superstitious about this room opposite me. The new patient is an old man whose cries are like a wounded animal's. It has taken two nurses over half an hour to ease him into quiet.

Sunday Wide awake again at half-past four and read till breakfast time. Sensitive young Sister Lark says he really is not in pain. He is mentally ill. For years he has been very much Big Business. Now, after being in command for so long, he can't accept things as they are. They can't sedate him any more than they are doing because, as it is, they have such difficulty in feeding him. But mightn't refusing food be Nature's way out? How is that poor old man any better served than a goose that is overfed when it has no future except as pâté de foie? More and more of these thoughts eat like moths into this long dark winter tapestry.

Monday They tell me the sergeant-major is leaving in ten days. It never seemed likely she could stay the distance of three months' probation.

Last night a young emergency nurse sister had the bad luck to find me in strife when she came on duty. A good brandy and tablet an hour before played me false. She was unsure about giving the injection she thought necessary. She left me saying she would be back in a few minutes. She may have contacted Matron, for very soon she was here, needle in hand, and with a wonderful touch gave me that thrice blessed injection.

Tuesday Miss Norah, fully dressed, hatted and gloved accompanied by Sandra, came to my room and sang me the first verse of 'Believe me if all those endearing young charms.' Perfect pitch, and by some miracle, at eighty-five, one of the sweetest, truest small voices I've ever heard. Her Dublin Irish diction, in itself, is music. Usually, night and day, she is strapped in, to prevent her running away. Yesterday Helen met her on her way out of the drive and brought her back. The pity of it. The pity of it. Born fifty or sixty years later, that lovely voice would have been heard. And not just on radio or T.V.

Friday⚇ 1°C this morning. I breakfasted in two warm dressing-jackets and my electric blanket at its top. And then was not a scrap overheated.

Sunday⚇ Watched the birds courting in the magnolia this morning. They looked too big for sparrows. Could they be thrushes?

This afternoon, Peter took me, by request, for a walk outside... angina.

Monday⚇ The new charge sister says to call him Matthew. I doubt if he will measure up to Peter, who is only here part-time because of his tertiary studies. While Helen and I were talking this afternoon the door suddenly opened. Mrs Douglas. Without speaking, she insisted on putting her clock on the already overcrowded small chest by my bed. She then turned to the bed saying, 'My daughter Sarah is in this bed,' and ripped the covers off me. Very gently, and I hope persuasively, I told her that this was my room, and this was my bed. By way of reply she picked up my lacy pink shawl saying, 'And this is Sarah's too.' At last she let Helen lead her back to her own room across the hall, but she insisted on leaving her clock here. She has a frenzied look today. But when she is not like this she is a gentle, very charming woman.

Tuesday⚇ A small triangle of sun on the wall at the foot of my bed, this morning. But still icy cold. And no birds singing.

Yesterday, Miss Norah, hatted and gloved as a lady

should be, ran away again. Searching in opposite directions, they at last caught her a couple of tram stops away, just as the conductor was putting her off the tram, because it was travelling in the opposite direction to the way she told him she wanted to go.

Four a.m. Mrs Douglas is talking audibly and insistently at my open door. Evidently fully dressed, with wooden heels tap-tapping on the uncarpeted floor, she walks up and down till Nurse takes her to her room again.

Wednesday Last night's angry wind is still fitfully raging. That promise of an early spring a few days ago was mere flirtation.

My outings have not been a success. Today, generous, steadfast Helen knocked my one small footstool of hope from under my feet. There's no other way but staying on here.

Miss Norah escapes, again. Much drama. She is found, having walked miles from here. So would I if I could.

Thursday In less than five minutes someone has opened and closed my door four times. No answer to my 'Who is there?' It must be some kind of compulsion – like coming into my room at two o'clock in the morning and switching on the big overhead light and waking me. Minutes later she switches it off and departs without answering my startled 'Who's there?' Someone prowling. Soon a nurse runs down the corridor and retrieves her. I slip one of the tablets, 'as directed', under my tongue ... I lie wondering. It is still quite dark, but nearly morning. Then, at last, sleep. And forgetting.

Friday My best of all doctors is visiting another patient here. Before he goes, he makes me an unofficial visit. That smile. A handshake. A word or two about Dylan Thomas. In a special way, he's our poet. I begin to understand why Helen says: 'He has only to put his head around your door and you're well.'

Saturday⫘ Yesterday, Miss Norah ran away again, as ever, towards home. Another great hue and cry, including police. A relative found her miles away, and drove her back here. Escapism seems to be her only foible. If they took her home she would probably try to run off to Milan or Florence. A hundred years ago she would have been in her own home, with a devoted maid and housekeeper or relative to care for her. Then she would simply have been an amiable eccentric.

Helen to see me and Doris G., just home from her jaunt across Europe. She brought me a delightful bunch of daphne from her garden and lively talk as well, of the boulevardes and Paris in the spring.

Friday⫘ These nights don't bear talking about. Their thrust is too deep for tears. Helen comes with daffodils I have never seen before. Mandarin- coloured fluted cups, each with five leaf-like petals of that pale incomparable yellow. Just the three look exquisite in the light amber specimen vase Lucy gave me years and years ago.

Tuesday⫘ Miss Norah has her heart's wish. After three escapes she has gone home to live with her sister.

Another conveyor belt visit from my G.P. At home he never made me feel less than a human being. I don't like his nursing home technique. And even more, I'd hate a novelettish 'bedside manner'. But I don't enjoy being de-personalised – is there such a word? And this otherwise very pleasant young man has no time to communicate.

Thursday⫘ This morning the old man opposite,

who for weeks hasn't spoken one word, shouted, 'Nurse, Nurse' for fully five minutes, with the strength of ten. He then hammered on his bedside table with something metal until a nurse came. Then in a very loud and clear voice he enquired, 'What are they charging me a day in this bloody place?'

August

Monday Another of those nights. After over four months I don't think I can take very much more. If I used ear-plugs I couldn't hear music, or the sound of rain, or of the birds at first light.

Think. Calmly. This little hospital is really meant for them. Not for you. Remember you're a terminal case. Prince Edward's couldn't keep you. In a way, you are here by grace and favour. But this row of private rooms grows more and more like a refractory ward, and never-ending.

Spasmodic pain in my arm again. 'Sister' Matthew came when I rang. He can be insolent, with a kind of paternalism which may be his peculiar way of caring. He was certainly very quick with the injection. I think I know how a whale must feel, now, when the harpoon hits it.

Tuesday Helen comes with fruit, more daffodils and two new paperbacks. It is still cold and squally. But next door their wattle is in full blossom.

Monday These hideous nights go on. Not an inch of any curtain or carpet to deaden sound. The lightest footsteps, even at a distance, can be heard. All the doors close noisily, but this could be necessary to give warning of these sad, determined, vain efforts to escape.

Tuesday I'm sure there's such a thing as self-euthanasia. Without help of any drug. One comes terribly close to thinking of it. I don't want to live, if this is the only way of living left to me.

Thursday A dramatic sunrise. Like a Turner that an expert art-dealer would call a fake. For me it is a happening. There's a kind of healing in nature.

Sunday This morning Sister Lark says that a great part of poor old Mr X's trouble is that he was promised he would never be kept alive to the point of mere existence. At times he is aware that this promise has not been kept. And now he is not capable of making the formal decision to ensure that his wish is carried out.

Monday Try as I will I can't throw off the long weariness and fret of the last few months. In a different way I'm just as disoriented as my mentally sick neighbours.

There's no love or thanks enough for Helen for all she is and has been to me. And I'm not unmindful of those golden friends who still come to see me on days when I'm the worst of company. But this happy exchange is only for a couple of hours a day. There are still all the other twenty or so tattered hours to be got through. In the meantime, like a shadow of Robert Herrick, 'I write of Hell: I sing (and ever shall) of Heaven, and hope to have it after all.' The kind of Heaven it must be is some place for terminally ill men and women who still have full control of their minds and senses. And still have some motivated living to enjoy, and something to give.

Thursday Nils to see me with a whole bag of my favourite Chinese gooseberries. He's much too generous. They are delicious. To myself, I seem poor in thanks for all these remembrances that for so long have come my way.

September

Sunday Nine members of our trial-and-error staff have left this week. Two of their own accord. The procession of day or night agency nurses continues. They are strangers and often at sea with no one here to show them around.

Today, I asked a permanent part-time sister who speaks my language, whether I might have a blindspot about our Charge Sister Matthew. After a brief pause came the answer: 'No. He's loved by all the patients and the staff – just as they loved Hitler.'

Friday The poor old man is still with us. Those harsh cries sound like a despairing, broken child. As if he's trying to say he is weary past bearing of this sham of living and all that goes with it.

Saturday Some of my increasing problems are due to the side-effects of a drug prescribed for me a year ago, and swallowed every single day since. Today, my special specialist has taken me off it. Forever.

And Matthew has suddenly left us.

Tuesday Dick came to see me today with a jar of grapefruit from his own tree. He had prepared it for me himself, with the complete gourmet touch. He is a marvellous human being. He always makes me forget the kind of things you can't bare your heart about. Like chest pain – that can make you think of easeful death – yet not for long. I don't believe that life is receding – yet.

Saturday Since Matthew's departure Matron has taken over his duties. Peace has broken out. Strange, but so easy and so pleasant.

November

Tuesday My specialist to see me again. Thrombosis.

Tuesday Nearly two weeks have passed and my ballpoint has been, unbelievably, a complete stranger. I was watching T.V. – a B.B.C. special programme about the House of Windsor. Fierce stabs of pain in my chest towards the left shoulder. A strange feeling in my head of nothingness. Almost like a blackout. But not quite, because I managed to ring my bell. No panic. But I did think this could be *it*. I'm not a praying person, but I remember saying in my mind, 'Please, *please* don't let me go until I see Helen again.' Brandy. A quick injection. Someone on either side, hoisting me up higher on pillows. Matron took care of me superbly. And a good young nurse, too. Afterwards, I glanced at the clock. It must have all been over in minutes – perhaps even seconds.

Sunday Last night on the air for the first time, I listened to Margaret Sutherland's enchanting *Calypso Carol*.

Flowing from the new owners and, especially from Matron, good old fashioned loving-kindness is seeping all through Journey's End. There's a return to some kind of happiness. The nights, at last, bring the gift of sleep. And those who so often leave us, go with dignity and peace.

Monday More thrombosis. No family Christmas tree for me this year. Veronica's famous roast turkey looks more and more like my blue duck.

The old gardener waves to me as he passes my open

door, 'Babies' weather' he observes – 'wet and windy.'

December

Wednesday✍ Between five and six this dark, grey morning in the garden next door, I can hear the lovely, liquid note of young magpies singing. I do hope they stay alongside us. Helen brings me some of the things on my list of Christmas gifts for the family and the staff. Next week she will bring gift-paper and help me wrap them – perfectly, just as she does so many things. I wish I could add to these a pack of worthwhile gifts for the jobless young.

Tuesday✍ Heatwave weather. Reading today about Cézanne. He says painting from nature is not copying the object; it is *realising one's sensations*. I couldn't have put is so well. But that is just what I've been trying to do, inside four walls, for nearly three years. No gleaning of wit, no transcendental chatter – just this one-way gossip. Now it must stop.

Tuesday✍ A whisper – no more – that sometime in the future patients will be able to take a telephone call from their beds. Inward calls only, but think of it. Garrulous me, for all these years, voiceless as a snail for so many long days, able, at last, to be within quick hearing of Helen, Veronica, Amanda or Kate. It means instant contact with one's own kind. And for me that is what survival is all about. There's life in this so long wished-for communication, and a healing-power that can do far more for most of us than all those so-called tranquillizers.

There's no official announcement yet. But this first-with-the-latest 'Bush Telegraph' is never wrong. It is no longer a question of 'if', but simply 'when'. It makes a wise, kind gift in compassion and enlightenment from the new owners for this coming year. Already I hear myself, as unexpected as an astronaut would be, saying 'Merry Christmas' to the family (by arranging an inward call from Helen) – from my own small box in outer space, as they come and go round the Christmas tree. Rapture even to think about it.

Christmas Day.♂ Life is still good – when you can see and hear. And what better place than Journey's End, with magpies singing, and a magnolia at my very door. To be waiting...

Virago

If you would like to know more about Virago books, write to us at 5 Wardour Street, London W1V 3HE for a full catalogue.

Please send a stamped addressed envelope

VIRAGO ADVISORY GROUP

OTHER BOOKS OF INTEREST

TESTAMENT OF YOUTH
An Autobiographical Story of the Years 1900–1925
Vera Brittain
New Preface by Shirley Williams

First published in 1933, this famous bestseller, acclaimed as 'the real war book of the women of England', is an elegiac portrait of a young girl's life in pre-1914 England, a heartbreaking record of the holocaust which followed, but most of all, a love story The highly successful TV adaptation of *Testament of Youth* won the Best Drama Series Award of 1979, and its star, Cheryl Campbell, Best TV Actress Award.

TESTAMENT OF EXPERIENCE
An Autobiographical Story of the Years 1925–1950
Vera Brittain
New Introduction by Paul Berry

In this sequel to *Testament of Youth*, Vera Brittain continues the story of those who survived the First World War, once again interlacing private experience with the wide sweep of public events. The story of her marriage, the birth of her children and her increasingly successful literary career are set against the panorama of one of the most stirring and crucial periods the world has known.

TESTAMENT OF FRIENDSHIP
The Story of Winifred Holtby
Vera Brittain
New Introduction by Rosalind Delmar

Testament of Friendship is the story of Winifred Holtby and the record of the remarkable friendship between her and Vera Brittain. Winifred Holtby died when she was only 37, at a time when her literary career had reached its peak with the publication of her greatest novel, *South Riding*. In her short life her generous, loving, talented nature shed a special light on all who knew her.

THE TAMARISK TREE 1
My Quest for Liberty and Love
Dora Russell

The remarkable autobiography of Dora Russell – educator, pacifist, socialist, campaigner for women's rights and second wife to Bertrand Russell. A portrait of an outstanding woman and a brilliant record of the century through which she has lived.

'A talented and courageous woman . . . her philosophy towards women and their potential is as valid today as it was in the 20s' – *Antonia Fraser*.

THE TAMARISK TREE 2
My School and the Years of War
Dora Russell

Dora Russell's second volume of autobiography tells the story of her life from 1935, after her divorce from Bertrand Russell, to the early years of the Second World War: a moving account of her personal and family life, her involvement in progressive education, and her struggle to run Beacon Hill School.

A DIARY WITHOUT DATES
Enid Bagnold
New Introduction by Monica Dickens

First published in 1918, Enid Bagnold's legendary World War I diary recounts her experiences as a VAD in a London hospital. This portrait of human suffering is a permanent memorial to the men who fought, suffered and died, and a moving cry against the callous horror of war.

'An extraordinary book' – *Evening Standard*

ROUND ABOUT A POUND A WEEK
Maud Pember Reeves
New Introduction by Sally Alexander

From 1909–1913 the Fabian's Women's Group recorded the daily budgets of thirty families in Lambeth living on about a pound a week. Poignant, moving, evocative – a classic account of working lives before the First World War.

'Their painstaking and sympathetic account is still heartrending' – *Guardian*

'I should like every employer and every trade union leader to have a copy' – *Methodist Recorder*

LIFE AS WE HAVE KNOWN IT
By Co-operative Working Women
Introductory Letter by Virginia Woolf
New Introduction by Anna Davin

'A classic account of the lives, aspirations and experiences of working women, whose recollections go back to the 1850s' – *Fay Weldon*

'One of the best, the most beautiful and most true books I've read for a long time' – *Bryan Robertson, BBC Critics' Forum*

'It has all the inspirational quality Virginia Woolf found in it nearly forty years ago' – *Jackie Gillott*

MATERNITY
Letters from Working Women
Edited by Margaret Llewelyn Davies
New Introduction by Gloden Dallas

This remarkable book, first published in 1915 and unavailable since then, presents, for the first time in their own words, the working woman's view of maternity. An historical document of great importance, this famous book is a moving record of courage, endurance and love.

'Do publish those letters, they are so amazing' – *Virginia Woolf*

'I found the total effect overwhelming' – *Elizabeth Longford*